Home
Grown
Enemies

ISBN: 978-1-4251-6952-7

We at Trafford believe that it is the responsibility of us all, as both individuals and corporations, to make choices that are environmentally and socially sound. You, in turn, are supporting this responsible conduct each time you purchase a Trafford book, or make use of our publishing services. To find out how you are helping, please visit www.trafford.com/responsiblepublishing.html

Our mission is to efficiently provide the world's finest, most comprehensive book publishing service, enabling every author to experience success. To find out how to publish your book, your way, and have it available worldwide, visit us online at www.trafford.com/10510

www.trafford.com

North America & international
toll-free: 1 888 232 4444 (USA & Canada)
phone: 250 383 6864 ♦ fax: 250 383 6804
email: info@trafford.com

The United Kingdom & Europe
phone: +44 (0)1865 722 113 ♦ local rate: 0845 230 9601
facsimile: +44 (0)1865 722 868 ♦ email: info.uk@trafford.com

10 9 8 7 6 5 4 3 2

Home Grown Enemies is about—America—a work in progress. America: The great experiment has almost, come full circle, started with freedom, socialism, and bondage are the final stages.

Home Grown Enemies: Was inspired by the American people and our do nothing elected officials in Washington. Inside the covers you will read about what our representatives have done to America, and it is not good. We have not had a leader since Ronald Reagan, and it has taken its toll. We American's that work, and contribute our hard earned money to support the government are fed up with 1/3 of our tax dollars being wasted.

We have come to the conclusion that being an elected official is very similar to being a prostitute one sells their body, and the other their soul for a few dollars. We feel that the one that sells their body may be more honorable because, they did not swear on a Bible to be honorable!

Inside the covers of Home Grown Enemies: you will find a ton of constructive criticism's, and common sense solutions to the issues being talked about. There are many, and our representatives are not addressing a single one of them, by offering a positive common sense workable solution.

Here are a few of the challenges offered Washington, and go wanting. Waste, illegal aliens, Welfare, social security, and a host of other issues, we have listed 16 items of concern. You must read: Home Grown Enemies, is very interesting it covers subjects in a manner no one else has dared to. It simply says what most American people think about you elected officials.

About the Author

Kenneth Hoffman is a retired Metal Forming Technologist, Practical Engineer, Machine Designer, Tool Designer, and R&D Specialist in Metal Forming. He has traveled the world on 15 occasions. He has written 36 technical books on metal forming. Ken consults with a steel company, conducting seminars, and teaching metal forming techniques.

Ken has designed, and built 7 houses from the ground up, by his self each house is a different design, and unique. When Ken talks about from scratch, that means the concrete work, framing, roofing, electrical, heating, dry wall, siding, painting and every finishing detail.

Ken is married, and has raised 5 boys. Writing a novel is a new experience for Ken. He has had to learn many things about the English language, long forgotten, he is 72 years old, and has watched America go through many hardships.

We are at the crossroads at this time in history, and we need a change of the guard to bring America back, from where we have wandered off to. We need a real leader that can run this show called America. Ken has seen America come from a position of greatness, to arrive where we are today a floundering, dysfunctional, divided nation, with a corrupt government, and elected officials that don't give a damn.

Ken loves America, when he was traveling he looked at several countries in which to retire, a result of the exploration is, America is my home. God bless America!

America "the great experiment" is the greatest country in the world, so let us be thankful, and do what we can to keep it that way.

"Home Grown Enemies", the enemies within America's borders, was inspired by our Congress-men and Senators.

The elected officials have caused our government to be dysfunctional. In Washington the waste capitol of the world, they do nothing but bicker, and debate.

The Democrats and Republicans are both to blame, they have their own demented way of doing it.

Stop the waste, and we will have enough money to fund important programs. If our elected officials solved these three problems, we would not have any money problems. The three problems are, in this order of importance waste, waste and more waste.

Home Grown Enemies

America Burns While Congress Bickers

Kenneth Hoffman

Dedication

Let freedom ring
To the melding pot of the world and greatest
people on earth The American people

CONTENTS

Home Grown Enemies
Acknowledgements

This book was inspired by visiting with many people over many years, and many years of watching our elected officials perform. The results are not too encouraging most all of you I talked to said, they waste too much time bickering, debating, trying to be reelected and procrastinating. The matter of the fact is I feel that if asked to join the procrastinators club they would retire before they joined. America deserves better treatment then that. All of you indicated to me that we must demand more from our elected officials. We pay them to do a job. I would like to thank all of you for your input. I know that most of you will not know why I was picking your brain. Asking probing questions about how you felt about our elected officials, until you buy a copy of this book and start to read it. Again, thank you from the bottom of my heart.

This has been a real challenge but I feel a very timely endeavor. It is time to change the coarse America has taken. The path we are going down is the path to defeat! We will not accept defeat. "Dingy Harry" and the like can preach their, "we give up crap" all they want. But we cannot allow them to have their way and most of you indicated, we must stop them. Thank you for wanting them to change direction. Support our President whom we all elected. If I have forgotten any one please forgive me. I appreciate all of you, God bless you and God bless America.

Thank you Kenneth Hoffman

Foreword

When reading Home Grown Enemies I found it very interesting that what Ken wrote about our Congressmen and senators is what most people think of them. He says we have not had Good Representation in Washington for about 20 years, is time for a change of the guard. He says the money Washington collects is more than enough to fund all needed programs. Waste is the problem1/3 of the tax dollars is wasted.

Ken States the demeanor of the representatives must Change before the waste issue can be resolved. Ken asks, representatives what are you waiting for? He left no doubt in my mind about how he, and those he polled feel about you. I think what he said is correct because every time America has a problem you bicker, compromise and attach Pork to all funding bills and he asks, for what reason?

Ken says you are not alone when it comes to Waste President Bush is at fault because he signs the bill, this means he accepts it. He asks, otherwise why would he sign them?

Ken also states that the criticism he has, are meant to be constructive, he states I love America and simply want the Washington group to do what is right. He says to him it appears that you, just don't care about anyone but yourself. Ken describes you as delusional, demented, ludicrous, maybe Bi Polar and certainly Dysfunctional. He asks, otherwise why would you let these things happen?

Ken believes you representatives are destroying America and believes unless there is a change for the better soon we will be socialistic. He believes we are our own worse enemy. I agree! I enjoyed reading the book Home Grown Enemies, and Think everyone would gain a much better understanding of the problems in America.

MFBT Consultant Robert Himmler

⋘ ONE ⋙

AN OVERVIEW OF THE BOOK

We have two varieties of "Home Grown Enemies" the worse one being our elected officials in Washington. With their do nothing approach to solving the illegal alien problem, SS problem, cost of medical care, Tort reform and balancing the budget. Plus many other things that require solving. Getting rid of the federal debt must be the top priority. With 1/3 of our tax dollars wasted, if the waste is eliminated, that will take care of all of our funding problems. Unless we get rid of the idiots we have in Washington it will not happen. Readers Digest has an article in the January 2008 issue that says it all. Titled "You've been had", "How the government wastes nearly $1 trillion of your money every year." We urge you to get a copy of it, the article is very interesting. We believe $1 trillion looks like this, $1,000,000,000,000 and that is 1000 X $1,000,000 = $1,000,000,000 X 1000 = $1 trillion. One cannot imagine this much waste. At least I cannot this is a lot of waste, a full 33% of our tax dollars $$$$ wasted. Wow! Washington is doing a much worse job then we thought. We don't believe Readers Digest would put this in print unless they made sure it was a fact. This article is, "by Ryan Grim and Joseph K. Vetter" I read the article on 12/10/2007.

Our public officials say public service is a noble profession. I agree with them, if the server is honest. Most are not otherwise we would not have the problems we have. We believe that most public servants are like those that practice the oldest profession in the world, both sell their bodies and souls for a few dollars. The first "home Grown Enemies are in Washington. We say this because they do not take good care of our interests. In fact they squander our resources with abandon. It is not a matter of increasing the tax like the democrats want to do. They would just increase the spending, to consume the increase. This happened many times before. Just so you understand the democrats are not alone. The republicans are just as bad. No one in Washington really gives a damn. All they care about is to get reelected to the part time job with the lush benefits.

It is not a matter of leaving the spending alone or reducing it. It is a matter of eliminating the waste. Not one candidate talks about eliminating the waste! Waste is the real problem it is the major cause of the federal debt. What fools we have running our government. That goes for both democrats and republicans alike. Both groups are guilty, they must agree in order for things to happen good or bad. Also it is not an across the board 15 % cut in domestic spending. Like Rudy Giuliani says he would do if elected. He just doesn't understand the problem is waste. Not an across the board cut in the programs. Some programs cannot have a 15 % cut, they maybe under funded now. They just don't get it on either side of the political fence. The waste comes in many forms, like programs and committees that were created years ago, serve no purpose, and have a life of their own, get rid of them. Pork is waste, overpayment to Halliburton and other contractors. No or inadequate oversight in all areas of the government. What a mess!

The second "Home Grown Enemies" are the Muslims that are born and raised in America. They go to the radical Islamic schools in the U.S.A. do not assimilate. Instead they follow the teachings of the radical Clerics in the mosques. In the U.S.A. 26 % of Muslims that claim to be American's are 18 to 29 years old think suicide bombings are justified. If they are in defense of Islam, this is crazy! The Koran does not teach separation of church and state. It considers the Mosque and the state one. In fact the laws of the Muslim countries are taken from the Koran. They are called Islamic laws. We must respect the right to religious freedom. Providing the religion does not advocate radicalism which is defined simply as (strapping on an explosive laden vest to blow up people). It cannot get more radical then that! Also they must assimilate, that means that they learn English. We must not allow our laws be changed for them. One example is the noise ordinance in the Detroit Michigan area. They make loud noises 5 times a day in the name of a call to prayer. If we Christians wanted to make a loud noise like that, people would be screaming about it. So we ask what do they not understand about assimilate? When a religion advocates the activities of radicalism we must defend our nation's people from them, with whatever means is available, Include listening in on private conversations. I for one would rather be listened to, then dead. If it will save my life or someone else's life, invade my privacy, please.

The solution to that is in Washington, allowing electronic surveillance. This way they can be caught and gotten rid of. Many of our Washington officials say if we do surveillance, we are invading the privacy of our citizens. Well invade my privacy. But please catch these radicals before rather then after the fact. We have enough copycat wacko radicals of our own. Let's get rid of those that live in America and don't like us. Also we must get rid of all illegal alien's, and close our borders so radicals cannot sneak across them. When Muslims were surveyed, all most half of them said, they do not believe that mostly Arabs carried out the 911 bombings. So what did we expect them to say? It seems that "the more things change the more they stay the same." The events that led up to the 2nd world war are repeating themselves today. Hitler was saying we are peaceful, we want peace. If you don't believe it just take a look at the radicals developing Nukes. Saying they are for peaceful purposes and most of the world saying. Let's use diplomacy and negotiate to find common ground. Our comment is we believe that there is no common ground. The radicals take your giving into their ways, as a sign of weakness.

All they will do is expect more. All one need do is look at what Clinton got Israel to offer Arafat in Palestine. When something was offered, they asked for more. They never agreed to do any of the things expected of them. The *"thank you"* was to rocket Israel to cause turmoil. Then in turn demand more, you cannot satisfy them. We mentioned earlier on their goal is to have it all. Even if that means *having to kill you,* so be it. Not a *single group* of Muslims has denounced what the radicals do. In fact when asked if it is *ok to kill Americans*, a great percentage of them say yes. The *Infidels deserve* it for interfering with Islamic affairs.

Then we have China, Russia, Cuba and others in the world that wish for the downfall of America. With "Dingy" Harry Reid and his group are their cheer leaders. If they will just leave us alone our leaders will destroy us from within.

They are working on our kids through the educational system and with the liberal education in the collages. It is a shame that most collages are liberal, but they are. This is starting to spill over into some high schools in the more liberal parts of the U.S.A. An example: in the Denver Colorado area, where a teacher "Jay Bennish" is teaching that capitalism is "an economic system at odds with humanity." America is the "the most violent nation on earth." He said Bush's 2006 state of the union address "sounds a lot like the things Adolf Hitler used to say." This took place at Overland High school, a Denver suburb. This is another "Home Grown Enemy", there are many more, just look around. Anyone who abuses the system by getting welfare they don't deserve, Social security benefits they don't deserve are part of the problem.

Then we have the group that determines what our new coins will look like. The particular one I'm referring to is the new Presidential dollar coin. This coin is one of the first steps, to removing God from our lives, it does not have, "In God we trust" on its face, instead "In God we trust" is on the rim. Do you know how well that will last? Look at a Quarter that has been around for a while, the edge knurling is worn off of it. Two points to be made, one out of sight out of mind. People's memories are short and who looks at the edge of a coin? Second point, the inscription will soon be worn off. Then when you look at the edge of the coin "In God we trust" will have been removed thru time and wear. This is a subtle-sneaky way to remove God from our money, and our lives.

Then we have this radical atheist filing a law suite in an attempt to get God removed from our money, and pledge of allegiance. This is another attempt at removing "one nation under God" from our pledge of allegiance, and from our money "in God we trust." Come on now we cannot leave one individual tell the rest of us how to do things. Yes he can believe what he wants, that's his right and his business but beyond that, we say bull crap! Our courts need to throw out these radical nonsensical law suites. They make a joke of our system of government. This is another "Home Grown Enemy." Our country was founded on Christian principles and removing God removes those principles. The people that advocate the inscription being placed on the rim of the coin rather then the face are "Home Grown Enemies" also. This is bad news, and this must not be tolerated. The majority rules not the minority.

Then we have good old Russia and their smiling leader that would, just as soon kill us, as look at us. We better not turn our back on that one. Russia has reverted to communism/socialism plain and simple. They have an agenda and are in cahoots with the radicals. Putin is getting them to do his dirty work. If the truth were known, he is doing all he can to keep the oil prices high. Then we have the addition of the Chinese balance of trade deficit an attempt to help bankrupt America. Putin and the Chinese have the help of our elected officials with their lethargic ways. Then we have the French whose butt we saved several times. They feel we owe them something, the Germans who started the 1st and 2nd world wars. These countries could give a darn less about what happens to the U.S.A. In fact we believe all three of them are selling war materials to the radicals. Since I wrote this the French and the Germans seem to be more pro America. They have elected new pro America leaders. Hopefully this is a lasting trend.

Then we must not forget the abusive Chinese. They use our markets to finance their war machine. We believe they are selling war materials to the radicals also. Now with friends like this who needs enemy's? Oh there are some more that are doing the same thing. They are in South America or North Korea and other parts of the world. The net of it is, we have a real challenge on our hands and do not have the leadership that is required to get the job done. When we speak of leadership we're speaking about all of those in Washington, it takes the whole group, to pass muster on any bill before any action can take place.

We must not forget our pork barrel president. He has allowed more pork to slide thru the cracks then any other president in our history. We understand there were 6,000 pork barrel attachments that were allowed to pass without a veto in 2005. I'm told there were 16,000 in 2006 with no veto. 2007 is on track to set another record for pork. Bush finally started vetoing bills he disagreed with late in 2007. Why was he waiting? 12/20/2007 I just found out that the defense bill Bush signed has 9,800 pork projects attached to it. Bush complained about it, but signed it. He signed it, that tells us who-what he is. I will defend most of Bush's actions, and I do support him. I voted for him, would do it again with the same circumstances. I'm disappointed in him. He is our president, but that does not make what he has allowed to happen Ok. We just do not understand why he allowed this to happen. This is enough spending of our tax dollars for foolish things. Why didn't he go on TV and ask the people for help to get the pork removed from the bill? We would have put pressure on our officials to get them to remove the pork. Wouldn't we? In fact many of those in Washington are America's worse enemies. Bush is a good part of the problem because he is our President-CEO, and that is where the buck stops. Many of our elected officials are bad news they say the war in Iraqi is lost. They try in every way possible to bankrupt America. By attaching pork projects to funding bills that are important, other wasteful spending, and by allowing American companies to move our jobs overseas. They are removing America's industrial base by allowing American companies to move our manufacturing base of critical items off shore.

They are allowing China to flood our market with cheap products, this takes away American jobs. Plus the trade China does with us is not fair or equitable for both parties. Many of the products are of poor quality, shabby at best and the sanitation they practice is horrible. *Trade is not fair,* when *one party gains* more then the other. It must change so it is *equitable for both* or be stopped completely. This brings us to the part where *each of us must do, our share "to unite America."* If we do not, then *we will certainly "hang separately"* it is up to us American citizens. Our leaders are not up to the job. Our leaders are preoccupied, with debating, bickering, earmarks (pork), getting reelected and procrastinating rather then serving America. About 95 % of the people that we talked to, indicated to us, they felt, the officials in Washington are our big problem. They cannot get together to take care of business. A good example of how Washington should function like a team is when the representatives are voting a raise for themselves. They are all in agreement, they are not Democrats or Republicans, and the vote is taken quickly. Passage is a sure bet! How would you like to be able to count on automatic raises? Wages have been stagnant for most American's, but not for Congressmen or Senators. Being a legislator on Capitol Hill guarantees pay hikes unless they vote to stop them. They never do! Want a great deal on health care and pension? Get a job on Capital Hill. As was stated in the book *"What's going on"*, wouldn't it be nice if we all had the same benefits. Like those that are supposed to serve us?

Guess who pays for all of those benefits? We tax payers do. No problem they just appropriate more of our tax dollars$$$$, to cover it. Members of Congress also get an annual raise tied to inflation. It took them 11 years to increase the minimum wage. No: it is not tied to inflation like their increases are. Not bad for a part time job. The whole point being they need to get real and live like we normal American's do. There is a limit to all things in life contrary to what they believe.

Common sense solves 99% of all problems but we apparently only have about 5% or less of the people in Washington with *common sense*. So we ask how does the job get done with a complete lack of what is required? The answer is it doesn't get done. That's why we have the problems with #1) No fiscal control and waste. #2) the legal system is crazy. #3) the representatives do not work. #4) Welfare is out of control. #5) Our representatives think talking will solve all problems. #6) No manager for America. #7) Our educational system sucks.

#8) Illegal aliens are a major problem. #9) Medical tort reform must happen. #10) Fair tax and no IRS. #11) The energy problem. #12) The abortion issue. #13) Drugs and drinking. #14) Fuel economy. #15) Politically correct. #16) Leadership and Reagan quotes. The items listed are but a few of those requiring attention, but they are the big problems and we have numbered these items, so we can refer to them by number as we go forward, so let's look at each of these items now.

TWO

NO FISCAL CONTROL—WASTE

#1) Have you ever heard the loud sucking sounds that take place when we send the government our tax dollars? That sound is 1/3 rd of our tax dollars going down the black waste hole created by our elected officials. We only hear about the overpayments to contractors that hit the news, most are hidden by the group of waste full, experts at cover up in Washington. We do not have a money problem, we have a waste problem. With wasteful run away spending, with no one tracking the money spent. The oversight of government programs sucks! Are not my words, these are the words of many of the young people we talked to. They are right on with that statement they said the whole bunch in Washington sucks! The government spending and waste has us and our grand children so far in debt that it may well cause the U.S.A. to default. If we don't default, it will be because our creditors took over the U.S.A. and thought it is better, if they leave it intact that way they can make more use out of it. When this happens, all people will become servants of the state. You can laugh if you want, but every country in the history of the world, that allowed a situation to develop where ½ of the people, supported the other ½ the system failed. Our government has 58 % of us supporting 42 % of them. They are the people on welfare, SS disability, retiree's with legal SS, illegal alien's, government workers, elected officials and yes the IRS. The IRS is the largest employer in the world, and is included, they work for us. With the baby boomers retiring soon the numbers will change drastically, this will tip the scales where the balance will be over the hump. Bad news!

Anyone that does not manufacture a product, provide a service to industry or create something of value for the private sector is being supported by us. Making believe you are doing something like our officials do does not count as being productive. We have the leading Democrat candidate, trying to buy votes by saying. We need to give every child born in the U.S.A. $5,000.00, that we need to raise taxes. Share what we work for with others that don't or are too lazy to work. This way we will all be equal, and we need to provide medical insurance for everyone in the U.S.A. When this person says everyone, she means the illegal aliens are included.

This way she will get their vote. Our question is what vote? An illegal alien gets a vote? I thought you at least had to be an American citizen to be able to vote, and if you were a law breaker, a felon you could not vote, even if you were an American citizen. We understand that a felon does not, or at least is not supposed to have the right to vote. Hillary is trying to buy the welfare, and illegal alien votes with our tax dollars. By promising the people that do not contribute a $5,000.00 payment for each child they have. Crazy! The point is, regardless of where the money goes, when the numbers reach a tipping point, the whole works fails. We are knocking on that door. If we do not get a handle on the illegal alien problem, it may well be the straw that broke the camels back, that along with the retiring baby boomers that deserve the SS benefits they earned. Why on God's earth are we supporting criminals? Yes illegal aliens are criminals: we understand that if you break the law, you are a criminal! At least that is the way it used to be. Let's get with the program and solve these problems before it is too late.

Stop the waste and control the spending. All credit cards have a limit, if you do not believe me, simply use your credit card, with no consideration about how much you spend then tell the credit card company, you want to spend more. Just how well do you think they would receive that? We expect the answer would be, you have a problem, and that will not work. We have our representatives spending our tax dollars, with no consideration. Yes they are using the government credit card, with no regard or consideration of the limit or the consequences. One day, some how, some one has to pay what is owed. If what is owed is not paid when it is due. The entity that owes the debt must either default or declare bankruptcy. We think the only way the rep-resentatives would learn how this works, is if one of us were allowed to manage their personal finances for a year. We would spend their money like they do our tax dollars. At the end of the year, give their personal finances back to them, in the same condition they have the government in. How do you think they would like that? Do you think they would understand? Why we feel the way we do, about what they are doing with our tax dollars-resources? They will never allow us to do this. But there is a way we people can get the job done. When you read the rest of the book you will see how we can do it.

Then we have what we call the fluffy dollar, the fluffy dollar simply put is. When our government starts the money pump, every time there is a money problem, to print more dollars, this decreases the value. They put a name on this practice to glorify it they call it monetizing the economy. In other words printing more money to cover their screw ups. This is the practice they used recently, to try to bail out the lending institutions that were not prudent lenders. Why should we have to pay the piper for lending institutions that were not prudent? Then they lower the interest rate to save these companies that did not do a good job. This stifles savings, forces more money into the stocks in companies that have not increased in real value. 1+ 0 does not equal 2, except when it is imagined, so if we print 1 dollar for every one we have now. Without creating value, we have inflation. God forbid that the fluff (fluffy dollars) that are in the economy catch up to real value. Real value is property or some valuable item or asset that is used to support the dollar. When the real value is not increased proportional to the number of dollars the value of each dollar is less. When inflation catch's up to the real value of the dollar it will be worth about 60 % of what it is now, overnight.

Each time the government does this, we retired folks are hurt because we do not get the automatic raises, like our part time elected officials do. We cannot gamble with our savings in a volatile stock market, if the market goes south, we are in deep trouble. When a person is older, they do not have time in their favor, to allow them to recover. So if something happens to diminish their net worth, retirement may not be too comfortable as a result. Stop trying to give our tax dollars away like you have been doing. Get some sense, it is about time, and do it before you destroy us. Dam it stop making fluffy dollars, we cannot afford your nonsense. We must remember that about 1/3 of the tax money we send Washington goes down a deep dark hole never to be seen or heard from again. We have three things that cause the funding problems in Washington. They are in this order; Waste, waste and more waste. Stop the waste and we have plenty of money to fund all needed programs.

◄ THREE ►

THE LEGAL SYSTEM IS CRAZY

#2) the legal system is crazy. We have laws that say in plain English that if you disobey the law. By speeding 20 miles over the speed limit you will pay $50.00 not #10.00 or $20.00 but $50.00 like the law says. That is the law says this is what the penalty is, accept the law is written by a bunch of lawyers. This means it is written so it can be interpreted many ways, by who ever reads it. Have you ever seen a lawyer just write, do this and this happens? They will have about 10 pages to say something, where a normal person could get the same message across with one paragraph. So now we have a person, who disobeys the law by running a dog fighting, gambling operation. The law says for each offense, you will pay this penalty, which say equals 10 years in prison. That seems cut and dried to me. Now this person is not a normal run of the mill person like you, and I. He is a person of color, and a football player with money. This means he gets special treatment considerations? Why would this be allowed to happen? Because each law was written to say many things, they can be interpreted to mean many things, depending on the lawyer's ability to explain them, to satisfy the need at the time. That way there would be a loop hole, to allow a person of means, to get off easy. Depending on how good a lawyer they could afford, its all about money $$$$ plain, and simple. Here are a few examples of what we are talking about. They are pretty much typical, of what we can expect, when a person of means or influence does something wrong. In all three of these cases, we think these people got away with murder? We must not forget O. J., Ted K or Blakely. It is our feeling these three got away with murder, no they have not been convicted. Does not mean they did not do it? No!

You and I would not be given special considerations. But we do not have all of the advantages, of money, position or fame. This means we can not use the influence of our position or our money buy our way out of trouble. Let's take a look at several other cases where several Hollywood females were caught. They were drunk or on drugs and driving. This happened numerous times one served 82 minutes in jail and the other got 1 day. Now I ask you if you were caught doing these things. Do you think you would have gotten off this easy? No way! Three things are considerations when you are caught doing something wrong. One do you have money, two are you a public figure, celebrity or three are you a minority. Here is how they factor in, to determine the penalty for your offense. One way is if you have money, you can buy your way out. How? By hiring the best lawyer and tying up the legal system for a long period of time. This will wear them down, so you can get off with parole. If the offense is serious enough, your high priced lawyer can plea bargain, to get you a lighter sentence. Two, if you are an elected official you can claim immunity. By saying, I was going to make a vote on the house floor, like the Kennedy kid did. Plus you can buy your way out if you have the wherewithal to do so. You can use the power of your office, we the people placed you in, to get special considerations and a reduced penalty? Three if you are a minority, you can get the several preachers, and organizations that run around threatening businesses with boycotts to side with you, using the race card to get you off with a lighter sentence. There are several other patterns that get special consideration. They are if you are lazy, on welfare, a pervert, an illegal alien, a repeat offender, a minority, are on drugs and booze you can generally get off easy with a plea bargain.

Plus we pay for, a lawyer for these crooks, in the form of a public defender. If you do not fit any of these descriptions, are in the middle class, you are screwed. Then you are prosecuted to the letter of the law. Plus you have to pay for your own Lawyer. One thing keeps cropping up that really does not make sense to us, *plea bargaining*. We wonder why do laws get passed to bargain them a way? If the law states if you do this offense, you will be penalized this way. I wonder what part of this do the judges not understand? Of coarse we are not applying irrational reasoning. Like our Lawyers and Judges instead we're applying *"common sense"* looking at the letter of the law. If we have laws, why do we not apply them, like they are intended to be applied? We think the answer is obvious, if the law were to be applied like intended. There would be no wiggle room, for influence peddling or graft and the system would be honorable, honest and function well, rather then corrupt like it is now. Self serving, dishonest, power brokering, and greedy public servants are the problem. These people get their way because we allow it to happen. As you read on, you will be presented with a way you and I can change that. And change it must or we will go down the tube. We are at the crossroads.

FOUR

THE
REPRESENTATIVES DO NOT WORK

#3) our representatives do not work or if they do it is part time. When they do work, what they do is all screwed up. Constant bickering, debating *procrastinating,* trying to make the other person look bad, placing blame for something that doesn't work, does not get the job done. When they do spend time on the job too often it is to serve their own purpose. They spend their time finding a way to attach pork-earmarks to a funding bill. This way they can peddle influence, so they can get payola. Most of you agree with what is being said here. When we talked to you, you told us you were frustrated with the entire group in Washington. You did not single out the democrats or the republicans. In fact some of you told us that, if you put the whole bunch in a bucket and shook it up. When you dumped them out all you would see is the same crap. Most of the young people talked to put it this way, they suck! At this time the approval rating of the Congress is at 18% (we believe it is closer to 5 %) and falling. This means most people know most of you elected officials are essentially useless. These numbers are based on talking to about 400 people at the Wal-Mart stores, car wash and whenever we could. We talked to people while shopping and when traveling across the country in various states. Wisconsin is one of the states it is a staunch democratic state. In Wisconsin most people had the same opinion. You suck!

How can the largest business in the world function with this kind of poor management? The answer is obvious, it cannot. This you can see by the lack of a comprehensive bill to solve the SS, medical, illegal alien and waste among other problems. The 5 % number came from questioning hundreds of people in person over a one year period. Not over the telephone or selectively done so the numbers can be biased. This is done with many of the phone surveys. Most people expressed disgust about the performance of all elected officials, saying most don't give a damn. As long as they are not asked to do something that may be controversial they are laid back. One of the most controversial subjects is the illegal alien problem. By the way anything that will not lend itself to making them look good is controversial. Doing the right thing is always controversial to them. Let me give you their meaning of controversial, "any subject or act that will cost them a vote or make them appear not politically correct". This definition fits for most democrats and republicans alike. We're not sure when it will all end it is just that, the time to change things has arrived. If the change for the better does not happen soon it will be too late.

≪ FIVE ≫

WELFARE IS OUT OF CONTROL

#4) the welfare is out of control. Almost anyone can get on the dole—all you have to do is make believe there is something wrong with you. Another way is get one of the lawyers that know how to use our corrupt system to get what they want. They can get you SS disability or welfare even though there may not be anything wrong with you to justify it. These programs were intended to help needy people not greedy or lazy people. The programs were not intended for illegal alien's that are in our country. Welfare should not be given freely to those mentioned. Only about 10-15 % of those on welfare and SS disability deserve it. Let's get the rest of them off of the dole and put them to work. As it stands people that create products that contribute to the economy—pay taxes in America support about 42 % of you that do not. An interesting point here is every country where it was 50/50 failed. America is knocking on the door to failure, at this moment we are at 58-42 if we reach another 8 points we will find out if this is true. Oh you can talk your nonsense about how good the economy is doing all you want. Just look at the debt with all of those that are standing in the wings, wanting to retire soon, and the balance of payments debt with China and other countries. Then tell me America is healthy. Also the government unemployment numbers are all wrong. The reason we say that is when talking to people that work for many large companies that are contacted, while conducting business, here is what they tell me.

We have 50% of our people laid off, are on a four day work week. We are asking for volunteers to take a 30 day layoff. Many other companies say we are real slow but holding our own. Again we say the economy is all smoke and mirrors. If they keep lowering the interest rate, pretty soon they will be giving money away. You cannot sell houses to people that do not work. You cannot build houses that there is no buyer for, it don't work. Come on now where is the common sense? Bull crap is what it is! Here are several examples of what welfare does to people. Here is how it affects their thinking. When in a grocery store this little boy 4 years old was taking candy bars off the shelf, sticking them in his mouth. Then throwing them on the floor, we said to his mom why don't you stop him? So she said Johnny stop! He kept right on doing what he was doing accept now he had a smirk on his face. Next we said take his pants down and spank his butt so he understands. He can't do things like that! There were two young women with her and one said "yeah I bet" for some reason. The next thing said was, we "bet all three of you are on welfare," which they were. All three paid for their food with food stamps, then pulled out a big wad of cash, to pay for their cigarettes, and beer for their boyfriends. We stated there is no Honor in welfare, why don't you get a job? One said I would have to move to Springfield Missouri, so we said we will pay for your move if you will go. Get a job there, keep it and the same goes for the two of you to her friends, they said no way.

We went thru the pride and Honor talk with them then let it go. They still are on welfare, with several more fatherless babies to care for. This is how they increase their welfare income. When kids are raised on welfare, they have the attitude that it is owed them. Ever since President Johnson's great society (purchasing of votes with our tax dollars) we have more kids on the welfare rolls then ever. The irony of all this is, doing wrong things generally, takes less effort then doing right things. The wrong things perpetuate themselves thru generations. The welfare rolls just keep growing. The next generation feels it is a right, an entitlement, because they were raised that way. And our officials in Washington want it that way, so they can control the masses. They want people to be dependant on them. I for one say "by the people for the people." Washington just get the job done we pay you to do. Like place an Army on the ground and the few other things we cannot do for ourselves. Keep your dam nose out of our business, unless it is required to defend America. A good place for you to put some effort is to get those off of welfare that do not deserve it.

This is about 80 % of those on welfare that will keep you busy. Let's get it done. Now!

Another case is, a 16 year old girl, who was getting straight A's in school, and her Mom could not afford the $165.00 for her to go on a field trip with her class. I was made aware of the situation. Talked to the 16 year old with the school principle present about a way she could get to go. My wife and I help kids who do well, when we can afford to. When they commit to working off the debt, we make it easy for them to join their class on trips, it makes them feel good. In most cases they earn it by working with my wife or if a boy with me. In this case the girl was supposed to work with my wife to pay her debt. The girl called once after she got what she wanted, the next time my wife saw her she said "wouldn't it be nice if everything was free and no one had to work for things." That was the end of the discussion. My wife walked away disgusted, the girl did not do what she committed to. These two scenarios are typical of what welfare does to the people that get it. They are slaves of the state, in bondage, with at least 80 % of them not deserving the welfare. Most of them are able bodied lazy individuals with no pride or Honor. Again Washington, get up off your dead butts and do your job. We don't need to waste our resources on deadbeats.

Also our politicians are so generous with our tax dollars that they feel they can use them to support or buy the good will of other countries (international welfare) all over the world including some of them that hate our guts. They just have not learned that

47

a blanket of paper-money does not solve problems. They keep wasting our resources like the fools they are. Again all of you are not fools just most of you. Here is how you can find out if you are one of the fools, look in a mirror. You must be honest with yourself when you do, only you will know who you are. If you do not have a way to measure yourselves use this approach as a gage. If you have not attached a pork barrel project to a bill, so you could peddle the influence of your office, the people have trusted you with. You have not taken a trip or money from someone, or a group trying to influence your vote. If you have not bargained your vote away, then you are in the clear. If you have attached a pork barrel project to a bill, or bargained away your vote. Then you are part of the problem-dishonest, one of the fools that betrayed your country. You are a "Home Grown Enemy" because you are part of the problem. We people know that most of you are fools. It takes a majority of you to allow the wasteful spending-giveaways to happen. The blame here lies with you folks in Washington. You are not doing your jobs you are not American's for America. So change and become part of the solution. Now!

SIX

OUR REPRESENTATIVES
THINK TALK WILL SOLVE ALL

#5) Most of your failure to solve problems are, because you public officials feel that all that is needed to solve any problem is talk, (they call it diplomacy) talk in my opinion is simply air movement. You must act to get something done. A problem cannot be solved with *debate,* bickering or *procrastination.* A paper *blanket* (money) will not solve the problem. We feel Washington is staffed with self serving individuals we are fools for letting them do this to us. We deserve better. Speaking of fools, we have these politically correct people that feel, when we Water board an enemy combatant. We are torturing them? They never talk about *the Muslims beheading one of our soldiers.* Does this mean that *beheading is acceptable* to them? Why is what America does always wrong in their eyes? But what the enemy does is not talked about. We would rather get water boarded then beheaded. Beheading is final water boarding is not. Get your head out of the sand and face facts! Some one has their thinking distorted in a very sick way. Delusional? Have

49

you ever moved a large object with your talk (your mouth)? I don't think so you had to act to move the object. Action does the, job not words, stop talking, start acting and get the job done that is what you are paid for. IBM has a saying; "stop talking-start doing" Its time so lets get it done. Now! Quote: from former Virginia Governor Mark Warner, "Politics is the only business where doing nothing other than making the other guy look bad is an acceptable outcome."

⋘ SEVEN ⋙

WE NEED A MANAGER
TO MANAGE THE U.S.

#6) we need someone that can manage a large operation (the U.S.A.) we have not had one for a long time. The offering for the 2008 election is bleak on both sides most of the candidates offered, are career politicians. This offering is not what we need because it won't work. The career politicians from both parties only know how to do what they have been doing. And that don't work, we need a person that can manage the government as President. A career politician cannot do the job this is a well known fact from too many years of them screwing up the U.S.A. We only have one person that we feel is capable of doing the job of President that is Romney. With Hukabee or Nute as the vice president, this would swing the Southern vote to their camp. Unless they join forces they do not stand a chance because the southern Baptists will not vote for a Mormon? This election is a mess because America is divided, and almost everyone has a different opinion. Since we made the above statement, Thompson entered the picture, we listened to him

51

the other day, and if what he is saying is true then he would be a good choice. One problem people have with Thompson is he is too vague! The other problem is Thompson does not stand a chance, he is not electable. We all have heard them say good things before only to be betrayed. Thompson is saying exactly what needs to done. Most of the other candidates have not done this. If they say too much, then get in office, and do not do any of what they said. They will look like Carter, and we do not need anymore of that. I still favor Romney because he has the best success record, when it comes to running a business.

That may change when watching the debates to see, if he or others do the side step, waffle routine on issues. I have seen and heard enough to convince me that the best choice for President is Romney. Romney has a successful business background he is the only candidate that will be a breath of fresh air for Washington. All Washington has seen are carrier politicians. A carrier politician has no experience running a business. They are only capable of what they have been doing in Washington this has not been good for America. This is obvious, look at the mess they have us in. Jimmy Carter is a good example of what we are talking about. Those of you that do not know about Jimmy Carter, he was President after the country got shook up by the Richard Nixon Watergate scandal. Jimmy was a poor lost soul, who did know how to handle the situations he was confronted with. Iran was holding a number of our people hostage. Jimmy had our military try a rescue operation, it was so screwed up that it failed miserably. He did not know how to act to correct the screw up. This was the first of many bad things that happened during his tenure in the white house. Another was inflation, interest rates went to as high as 18-20 percent, what a mess he caused. Jimmy had the touch that no one wants, whatever he touched turned to crap. He was bad news for the U.S.A. we don't need anymore (Jimmy Carters) bad news.

Romney's background as a problem solver is good, he is the only person with a record of successfully running a business, is a matter of fact he has taken numerous troubled business's, and turned them around. He did the same thing with the Olympic mess he was asked to clean up. With the state of Massachusetts, it was deep in the red when he became Governor. He left the state with it in the black, and in good economic health. This was accomplished by a republican in a democratic state. This means he knows how to get the job done. We feel that Romney has common sense, will go to the people to get the help needed to pressure our representatives to do the peoples bidding. We the people must govern. To do this we need a leader that can pull us together to cause this to happen. We feel that Romney will do what is needed to get the job done. We have not had a president that talked to the people, asking them for support to get the job done, since Reagan. We do not need the hate America, *God* less career political figures that many of our representative's are they have proven they cannot do the job. The U.S. government is the largest business in the world, and for a long period of time we have not had a person in charge, that is capable of running a business. Let alone the largest business in the world.

At least the last three presidents were-are not capable and have done a lousy job on the domestic front with SS, the IRS, and many other things a mess. The illegal alien and many other problems go wanting for solutions. There is no end in sight as Washington is not capable of being honest. That is what it will take to solve these problems. Honesty! We need Romney as our president with Nute or Huckabee the vice president. This way the southern Baptist vote can be gotten, also each of these two have a good head, will complement the office. The southern vote is needed to give them enough votes to be elected. They are the only ones up to the job. Should this happen the U.S.A. would start back on the right path. They would go to the people and say hey folks we have problems we need your help. We need you to get your representative's attention. This is a bill that is part of the solution to get it passed we need them to vote for it now. I guarantee there is no pork in it. This is the kind of action that has to take place, to get the job done. We need a change because what has been going on has not and will not do the job. People empowerment, the people need to take control "by *the people for the people*" not by a few for the many. Speaking of not by a few for the many, something is wrong when a minority can get things to happen, but the majority cannot. We the majority, have to start making noise. When we do this we will be able to drown out the minority and we will start to get things to happen our way.

We have about 82% of the American people saying they believe in Christ and are Christians. We have a minority that want God removed from almost everything in our lives. We just do not understand how the minority is allowed to make decisions for the majority. The majority must make more noise. The squeaking wheel gets the grease. We just plain must step up to the plate and take charge for if we do not pretty soon. The minority will control what happens in America let's get with the program before it is too late. A good example is what is being done to remove God from our lives. The new one dollar coin has "In God We Trust" on the rim of the coin where it is out of sight. It will wear off like the knurling on a Quarter does. Then the next step will be to say why bother, it will wear off after awhile anyway so lets not waste the effort. This kind of activity by the Atheist minority must not be allowed to take place. We the majority must take control or it is one more step downward.

≪ EIGHT ≫

OUR EDUCATIONAL SYSTEM SUCKS!

#7) we used to teach the three Rs in school, reading, riting, and rithmetic but in recent times another R has been added. The fourth R is radicalism, it is taught in a few schools. When taught they openly declare capitalism "an economic system at odds with humanity." The United States is declared "the most violent nation on earth." This was taught at Overland High school in suburban Denver Colorado by a Geography teacher "Jay Bennish", he said "Bush's 2006 state of the union address sounds a lot like the things that Adolf Hitler used to say." Remember, these comments came in a geography class for 10th graders. The parents could not believe what their son was reporting to them. So the son starting recording the "Jay Bennish" lectures. What he was telling his parents was not believable to them, they listened to the recordings themselves then they were played for the principle of the Overland Colorado High School. She had not responded at this time, said to the parents when she heard the recording that "I doubt there would be any action taken." The teacher "Jay Bennish" was suspended for about two weeks then reinstated. It was noted, that the biased education that is taught in our collages, is filtering down into our high schools.

Another problem we have with our educational system, the testing method! All the school system is interested in is preparing the students for the next test so they look good. To hell with what the student learns. I know that the school in our area tutors the students specifically for the test. It appears to me that the school system thinks the test is more important then the general teaching-learning of the student. When I went to school the class was 30 to 45 kids and we were tested at each step of the process, on each subject taught. We were not tutored before the test, we were tested cold turkey. The test was hand written, not multiple choice tests like they are today. The testing was to see if we were catching on to what was taught. If we were caught cheating we were given a zero on the test. Now it seems that the SAT test can be doctored up to make the school look good. Many schools have been caught cheating. American Legion magazine has an article in the January 2008 issue that states. "Teachers have been caught showing students the answers to the questions." "And in some cases the teacher even changed the answers, after the fact to make the overall test scores look good." Can you believe that? We have talked to many teachers in numerous schools, many of those we talked to we would not want teaching our children. Some of them are fat, lazy and are not honest. Some of the things that happen may not be the teacher's fault the system may be at fault. All they are concerned with is how they look on a piece of paper, rather then what they teach the kids. We have several relatives that are teachers. We do not know how on Gods earth they got a teachers certificate. We do not know how they got certified to teach? Shocking!

Many of the younger parents tell us the school system sucks. These are their words, told us when we asked how they felt, about the school their children attend. They said that it does not address the problems, but instead will take a student that is active. Put them in the special education classes that were created to make it easy for a teacher to place a student they cannot handle in. In too many cases a student that excels is placed in the special education classes. The teacher doesn't know how to challenge them. The system wants all students to be equal so they can use a standard approach to all teaching. This won't work folks the good lord made all of us different. The problem here lies with the teacher's, and how they were taught to teach in collage. They are taught to be parrots of their professor's in collage. Most cannot think on their feet so they do what they are taught. This means they can only handle situations where every one-thing is the same. Not good at all! The conclusion, we have come to is, the good teachers are underpaid. Those that cannot think for themselves are overpaid, and maybe should be flipping hamburgers. This way they will work where every thing is the same time after time. We have the same situation in the school system, we have in the government, called the paper cover up. The people that run the system think money or paper solves all problems. They believe all you need is to pass a law, or throw more money at the problem and it will go away. It is called the paper blanket. They feel all one need do is cover the problem with a blanket of money and it will go away. The Chinese say America is the paper Tiger. Now how do you suppose they arrived at that conclusion?

The end result covering up problems rather then solve them. This is leading to what is called the dumbing up of America. The school system is doing a great job of it in most cases. The liberal teachings in our schools are one of the many things that will lead to the destruction of our nation if allowed to continue. The American Legion has an article in the September 2007 issue titled "Failing Grades" that tells all about what's going on in our schools. Read it if you can, it will tell you the true story about our school system. This story tells all about the tutoring for the tests to make the school look good. And the biased teaching with *"hate America"* its theme. We people must put the pressure on our elected officials, to stop this radicalism before it gets too far out of hand. I for one hope we are not too late. If we act now it may not be too late, we cannot expect our elected officials to do the job without pressure from us. They do not have the decency.

⋘ NINE ⋙

ILLEGAL ALIENS ARE
A MAJOR PROBLEM

#8) the illegal alien problem must be addressed. It is costing us an arm and a leg to allow them here. Contrary to what is being said, most of them are not paying taxes or SS. The people they work for may be taking it out of what they pay them, but I believe many of them pocket the money. Why do we say that? Just think about it for a minute, they have phony SS numbers. This means they are not registered, so there is no record of what takes place with the money. When phony SS numbers are used, the IRS would not know what to do with the money there fore it would be sent back to the sender. With the employer of illegal aliens knowing this, the question is, do they even bother to send it to the IRS? If you look at how the IRS functions, remember if you have an overpayment of your tax or SS. They will send it back to you with interest, because they want their books clean to the last penny if possible that is the nature of accountants. Also if you under pay they will send you a letter telling you why they feel you under paid. And what action you must take, I know how they function I have been on both sides of this story. The whole point here is *the illegal alien's do not pay their own way.* This makes them a burden that we must shoulder. Our elected officials in Washington are not handling the problem. Why not? 1/30/2008 I just found out that the stimulus package that our representatives have agreed to includes a tax rebate, for illegal aliens? What's wrong with them? This is crazy!

Because it takes something they do not have, honesty, spinal fortitude, they will not face the truth. If they do they will have to do something, and to do the right thing will cost them some of the Hispanic (illegal alien) vote. Yes we believe that some-most of the illegal alien's get to vote. In some states all you need to be able to vote, is a drivers license. Some states give illegal alien's drivers licenses. This tells the workers at the voting station, its ok for them to vote. On June 6th 2007, 33 of our U.S. Senators who pledged allegiance to the U.S.A. dishonored themselves. By voting against what 91% of what we American's want, English only for our official language. Four of these belligerent Knuckleheads are candidates for the president of the U.S.A. they are Biden, Clinton, Obama and Dodd. We do not need a person that betrays the people of America for our president. If for some strange reason one of these three is elected President, God save us! All of the 33 senators that voted against the English only bill are Democrats. Except the strange one Senator Jeffords of Vermont who betrayed us several years ago. One that is a real disappointment to me is Senator Lieberman, he voted against the bill also, we expected better from him. Now you can see why we the people must take charge, these Knuckleheads will betray us, to suit their own purpose. They really don't give a damn about America, but instead favor the illegal aliens over the American people. To us, they are traitors, and a disgrace to America we need to get rid of all of them.

This is a sad day For America. What in the hell is going on? Also our police officers are not allowed to ask a Mexican if they are here legally. Also they cannot ask if they are an illegal alien. My God what is wrong here? This is absolutely crazy. So we pay the price, for our corrupt official's ways one more time. This illegal alien problem must be addressed for security reasons. With our porous borders, Islamic radicals can enter our country. Let's close the borders, the cost to close the borders will be less, then what we pay for the illegal alien welfare, and medical cost. What is the illegal alien cost to tax payers? Here is the estimated cost to American citizens, $18,000,000,000 for welfare, $2,200,000,000 for food assistance, about $3,000,000,000 for medical care, about $25,000,000,000 for educating them and their children that are born in America. About $2,000,000,000 to jail the criminal illegal aliens we have incarcerated. And with the jobs lost to the illegal aliens, we lose about $210,000,000,000 in wages every year. The total loses to have them here to tax payers is close to $400,000,000,000 a year and growing. The cost to close the border and enforce our laws would be about $70,000,000,000 a year for about 3-4 years then drop drastically. The savings per year amounts to $330,000,000,000 this number is expressed, like Billion with a capital B. The reason we would experience this savings is when the fence was built that cost would cease. After that we would only have the maintenance cost. We must close the borders or pay the price every year.

Let's get a handle on this illegal alien voting question once and for all with a voter I.D. card. This card would have a picture on it, and a bar code so it is difficult to counterfeit. This card would also be used to determine if a person is employable. This would eliminate most if not all illegal alien problems because there would be no jobs for them unless they had the card. We cannot have people who disobey our laws be rewarded, by being afforded the privilege of living and working in America, or voting. If we disobey the law we do not get a reward, or is this, a new concept that is going to be practiced. Then applied equally to all American's, along with the illegal alien law breakers? Where is the common sense?

Here is how President Roosevelt felt about immigration in 1907. "In the first place, we should insist that if the immigrant who comes here in good faith becomes an American and assimilates himself to us, he shall be treated on an exact equality with everyone else, for it is an outrage to discriminate against any such man because of creed or birthplace or origin. But this is predicated upon the person's becoming in every facet an American, and nothing but an American. But something else also isn't an American at all. We have room for but one flag, the American flag. We have room for but one language here and that is the English language and we have room for but one sole loyalty and that is a loyalty to the American people". Theodore Roosevelt 1907. President Roosevelt does not talk about illegal aliens, but talks about people that come to America as immigrants. An immigrant is not breaking the laws of America, but illegal alien's are so we need to treat them like criminals because that is what they are. Get them out of America they are one of the elements destroying our country. When we decide, they can return in numbers determined by America, as immigrants, and before they can become Americans they must learn the English language. We are an English speaking nation, our tests to become a citizen are in English, and we must not change that for anyone. *We will defend the illegal aliens that choose to serve in our armed forces, when they have served several years honorably and learn English they must be given citizenship immediately.* Think about it they have put their life on the line for America, they have earned our respect, and their citizenship some, have paid the ultimate price for us. The only requirement that we feel is a must, is they must learn English, and must assimilate them selves to us, in order to truly be an American.

TEN

MEDICAL COSTS—TORT REFORM

#9) Medical costs are way out of line, and we're being told by some doctors that they pay upwards of $200,000.00 for an individual practice per year, and close to $1,000,000.00 per year when they own a clinic, for malpractice insurance. So if you think about it a hospital would pay even more then that for their malpractice insurance. Guess who ends up paying the cost of the malpractice insurance? You and I do, add this to the defensive medical practice doctors do, to try to defend against a malpractice law suit. Now you will better understand why our medical costs are so high. What is defensive medical practice? Defensive medical practice is what doctors do, so if someone sues them they can say. We did all of these tests to make sure, that what we did, was the right thing to do. That is why your doctor wants to run all of those tests, you may feel are unnecessary. The reason the malpractice insurance is so high, is when a malpractice law suit is filed, and the victim wins the case. The damages awarded are unreasonably high. This practice of a jury awarding damages that are not deserved is exactly how John Edwards became a multi millionaire. Tort reform is needed, so there is a limit on the amount of the damages that can be awarded.

If you read the newspaper, or listen to the news you will see, where a victim was awarded 10-20 or even 30 million dollars, plus medical costs for life. A lawyer will get 30% or more of the award. Ridiculous to say the least! We're being told if Tort reform was enacted, so the maximum award is $500,000 or less, most of the problem will go away, immediately. Texas has a tort reform law that limits the malpractice award to $250,000 or less. The effect of this was, to reduce the cost of medical care 20%, or more, immediately! Why? Because the lawyers are not interested, in taking a case where they will not get, the large windfall fees, like John Edwards did, which made him a multi millionaire. The number of malpractice lawsuits in Texas fell immediately. Along with the malpractice insurance, being reduced, most of the defensive medical practice is stopped. Only the necessary tests would be used to determine a person's condition, this would further reduce medical, and malpractice insurance costs. So why is Tort reform not enacted by our people in Washington? Money $$$$ plain, and simple, if they enacted tort reform they would not get the large amounts of money $$$$ from the lawyer lobbyists. We all know the people in Washington like money $$$$, more then America.

Tort reform would limit the award a victim received the result would lower malpractice insurance. The lack of a comprehensive tort reform bill is just one of two major reasons for high medical costs. The other is the high cost of drugs. This maybe a little harder to lower, but it can be done, again most of the problem is the people in Washington like money $$$$. If they go after the high drug costs, the drug lobbyists would not have, the large amounts of money $$$$ to throw at them. Another reason we have the high medical cost is the easy life we American's live, which costs somewhere between150 to 200 billion $$$$ a year and is climbing. Then we add the fact that we have accepted that being fat is ok. In fact the fat folks have started the pleasantly plump society, the robustly beautiful, and some other groups we do not know the names of. Matter of fact we do not know if we have these names right, but you get the idea. We have young people dying before their parents, in an ever increasing number from heart attacks, sugar diabetes, and other obesity related diseases. With the obesity rate in America at about 35 %, with about 25 % of American's fat, but not quite obese, it is no wonder, that we have a problem. All you need to do to see for yourself if this is true is, go to a Wal-Mart store, sit on one of the bench's Wal-Mart provides, and observe the people passing by for a half hour. Now you can see the problem first hand.

Be honest some of the folks are just fat, not quite obese yet, but they are working at it. We have an acid test for you to conduct. This test will tell you, if you are happy with where you are with your weight. To do this test get in front of a mirror, with all of your cloths removed, if you like what you see. Because you have no flabby rolls of fat, would not be ashamed of wearing a reasonably conservative bathing suit in public. God bless you, you are not part of the problem. Be completely honest *"And ye shall know the truth, and the truth will set you free"* (*John 8:32 King James Bible*) if you can say to yourself I like what I see "good" for you. We know that some of you have genes, or medical problems you are struggling with, that cause your weight problem. Do not feel bad, this is not meant for you. This is meant for the folks that cause their weight problem that will not take care of themselves for whatever reason. No I'm not the pot calling the kettle black I'm not fat let alone obese. Yes I have to work at it some of my medicines cause weight gain. You can do the same thing, all it takes is effort.

Add the cost of giving medical treatment to the illegal alien's. This has the state of California, Arizona, and several other states in a world of financial hurt. This tells you why we have high medical costs in America. In Washington two things are important money $$$$ and power. The people are secondary to them, or in this case third, on their ladder rung of importance. A large portion of the medical costs are "Home Grown" you can see that, which makes those that will not do anything about the problem, "Home Grown Enemies". This problem is on the shoulders of our elected officials, we know how they will handle it, or should I say not handle it. We do not need a socialized, second class medical care system, like some countries have. The medical care in those countries is not the best. How do I know that? Well, all one need do is ask questions about the health care in Canada, where they have socialized medicine. You will find out that when a Canadian has a serous problem, and can afford it they will travel to America for treatment. To get treatment in Canada may mean you are put on a waiting list. I'm being told that the care you will get, providing you are lucky enough to be treated is not the best, also that you may die while waiting, because the lists are long.

If our elected officials feel socialized medicine is the way to go, why don't they go to Canada for treatment? They don't go to Canada because America has the best medical care in the world. They have to know what socialized medicine amounts to, as far as quality, and service, so why would they expose us to, second best health care? If they feel that a socialized system is that good, they should go to Canada for treatment, when they are sick. Rather then use the doctors we provide for them. I know a little bit about the Canadian socialized medical system. I lived in Canada for a while, and was treated by the Canadian medical system. It is ok for most things like a cut, a cold, the flu and other normal health problems that life will deal you. But for the serous problems America is the best place to get treated, because we have the best doctors, and the latest equipment to do the job with, plus you can get treated in a timely fashion, rather then placed on a long waiting list.

⫷ ELEVEN ⫸

THE IRS—FAIR TAX A SOLUTION

#10) Fair tax is an interesting subject, and a cure for the nightmare we have now with the tax code. With the fair tax, all people in the U S A would pay 22 to 23% income tax. The tax could be filed on a small piece of paper that would fit in a 3 5/8 by 6 ½ envelope or on a post card. The only deduction would be charitable with a limit, a company would use a similar filing system with charitable, maintenance, capital expenditures, and R & D the only deductions. There would be no social security tax like there is now. The Fair tax would be the only tax you would pay to the federal government. All employees would have to be verified that they are American citizens. Everyone would get a special wire embedded card that would have a picture of the person on it. The card must be scanned to confirm they are employable a green card holder would have a similar card. The same card would be used to vote this would eliminate most of the voter fraud concerns.

A Federal sales tax would do the same thing, and may be a better choice instead of the fair income tax. This way all people would be taxed fairly.

The size of that mess called the I.R.S., the largest employer in the U.S.A., would be cut down to about 20 % or less of its present size. This would eliminate the cheating, and tax everyone equally. If you do not pay tax to support the country, you would not be able to vote. Why should a person that does not support the country, have a say in how the country is run? It is only fair unless you pay tax you don't get a vote. A voter card would be issued to everyone. The card would be embedded with wires, have a magnetic bar code, and the person's picture on it. This card would be scanned at the voting place or before being employed. Enough said as we want it simple and effective. There is only one problem I see with the federal sales tax, is it would tax the poor people equally. They could not afford to pay the 22 % added price, for items they bought that are basic needs to maintain their health. That would be taken care of with food, not being taxed at all. We do not want any paper work that causes any confusion, or added effort. If we start adding paper work, then there is an opportunity for cheating. We do not want to open that door, once we have it closed. The tax code would only require one or two pieces of paper, and be written to say that all products are taxed at 22% except food. A fair tax or federal sales tax solution is doable, either one will solve many problems.

＝ TWELVE ＞

THE ENERGY PROBLEM

#11 energy alternatives is an interesting subject, there has been a lot of talk, but no real good short term solution, presented to us by Washington. We feel that the *Alcohol from corn solution is a failed policy*, if we take all of the corn and convert it to Alcohol, we will only replace about 10 % of our gasoline usage. This will drive food prices thru the roof. At this time corn prices have increased about 30 %, soybeans about the same amount. The Mexican's are complaining their tortilla shell prices have increased, about 300 %. This is true since we started using corn, to make Alcohol fuel. The plan is to increase the amount of corn, we convert to fuel. This is crazy! Let's take a look closer to home, milk prices have gone from about $2.69 a gallon, to over $4.00 a gallon that is an increase of 33 %. As we increase the amount of corn we convert to Alcohol, other prices will follow real soon. Not a good solution at all, in fact it is a real problem, inflation will follow these price increases. Washington is saving the oil in the ground in Alaska, and along the coast of America for what? We just do not get it! All of the other countries drill along their coast. China has

72

signed an agreement with Cuba, to drill the Cuban coast. What are the people in Washington thinking, or are the arrangements at this time such that, they cannot get a cut of the pie? Well Washington, get with the *American's for America* program. We need real live solutions not *smoke and mirrors.* We have always said 30 years ago, and will say it again, why have we not increased the average mileage our cars get, by 20 %? This should have taken place 25 years ago it was doable then, and is doable now, without any real sacrifice. Looking at this approach, we would have lessened our use of oil for this purpose proportionally. Clinton had this opportunity, Bush had this opportunity, and we still are screwing around. The Hybrids are starting to make their way to the market this is a step in the right direction. The American people that care do not understand, why it takes so dam long to get the ball rolling. Damn doesn't Washington care, or not know how to do basic arithmetic? Forget the political bull crap, and get with the program. Also let's drill now as the problem is real, and immediate. What are we saving the oil for? Enough debate about that subject, let's drill. IBM has a saying "Stop talking—Start doing."

THIRTEEN

ABORTION

#12) Abortion is a subject that causes many people to get upset, because abortion like it is practiced is *Murder.* Let's take a look at an example of why we say that, before we describe, how we understand the partial birth abortion is performed. We have had several cases where young girls have become pregnant, had the baby in a bathroom, killed the new born, and threw it in a dumpster. They were tried for murder. Now we have a doctor perform a partial birth abortion, (here is how we understand the partial birth abortion happens) at birth the baby is about half way out of the birth canal, the doctor sticks a sharp instrument in the back of the babies head. Then the doctor uses a vacuum to remove the brain. This is not called *murder?* What else can we call it? The young girl killed her baby immediately after it was born. The doctor killed the baby one tenth of a second sooner, and it is not murder? Come on we didn't just get off of the turnip truck! We have a situation here where a person, and a couple of judges in the Roe V/S Wade case ruled, that it is ok to kill babies. This person has said, I was wrong, and abortion is wrong, at least she came to her senses. Now we ask when do the judges do the right thing, and come to their senses? *"By the people for the people"* not by a person, and a few judges for the majority! Most people in America feel that, all abortion is wrong. Except where it is a matter of life or death, for the mother, we agree.

We talk about humanitarian abuses in China, Africa and elsewhere. We believe there is a need to look at what we are doing, before we talk about what other countries are doing. Life starts at conception! The judges and other officials concern themselves, with how we execute a convicted murderer. They say the way we do it is not humane the person being executed may feel some pain. How considerate of them! We wonder where the concern is for the person, that was murdered or where their compassion is, for the little babies. Do they not have any feeling? Then we go to another extreme with some states, giving birth control to children young as 11 years old. The message sent them is heck kids go have fun, you cannot get pregnant! Not only do they do this, but they do it without the parents consent. Since when does someone else decide for a parent, what a child can or cannot do? Let alone something that is, unquestionably of an immoral nature, and may make children think being immoral is ok. Are we getting like Germany was, before the 2nd world war? Where the government, removed the children from the homes, so they could be taught, what the state wanted them to learn. This way they could control them? Our Collages are so liberal that talking about America in a good light is taboo, but bad mouthing America is cheered, and filtering down to the lower grade levels. We people need to get our dander up. Allowing this to continue will cause it to get worse. We cannot let this distorted thinking win out!

FOURTEEN

DRUGS AND DRINKING

#13) Drugs and drinking are a major problem to-day. They have been around forever. During the Vietnam era drugs became real popular, it is the belief that the main cause of this is the easy life. The parents wanting their children to have it easier than they did, so they gave them too many things they did not earn. This resulted in too much time with nothing to do. A result of this is boredom, this caused the kids to seek satisfaction-pleasure (or as they say kicks), in areas not explored before. After a number of years of peace after the Korean war (politically correct name police action) America got involved in the Vietnam war (early 1960s), which escalated considerably. The young soldiers that served in Vietnam were exposed to drugs of every description, while serving there, and got hooked on them. When their tour of duty was over, they brought their habit back home to the U.S.A. with them. This kicked off the drug culture, and America was not prepared to handle it, so it spread like wild-fire to the general population. Almost all kids were using Marijuana-pot in the late 1960s, this problem got worse in the 1970s, with about 98 % of high school kids using. Like the problem with too much time on their hands, pot did not give them the satisfaction they were looking for. They still did not know what they wanted a result was pot became a gateway drug. This brought them to trying stronger drugs, an attempt to find their purpose in life. Too late! Many of them were hooked, and were selling drugs to support their habit. With kids smoking cigarettes to look cool, it was easy to convince them that smoking pot was not really any more harmful. What's the difference? The comments we heard were; you can think clearer, you are more laid back, and much more aware of your self. One of their comments, is pot gives you that feeling of well being. Cool man! You could buy the stuff every where in Nickel and Dime bags, at school, on the street, and any other place you can imagine. The kids selling pot were creative they would even provide home delivery. Order a Pizza, and how much pot do you want? Many of the Pizza delivery kids were selling, it was natural to couple the deliveries up. How did the users know they could order Pizza, and get their pot? Word of mouth, they knew! Drug users took care of each other, because they needed to have a supply, and would keep each other informed. Pot being a mild drug led to; I don't get a kick out of it like I used to. Next step in drug use!

The gate was open, now we need more buzz, to do this requires a stronger substance. Here are a few; Coke, Morphine, Animal tranquilizers, Crack, Meth, snorting paint, and many others. The drug users are creative, they will try anything, so they smoke it, swallow it, inject it, cook it in their food, snort it and any other imaginable way, to try to get a bigger better kick. This leads down a road to nowhere. If they have a family it is soon forgotten, the drug users only love now is another high. Soon the law catch's them, now they have legal problems they go to treatment, and counseling. Their facial features change drastically, they age 10-20-30 years before their time, and some of them die with an over dose of drugs. Some die of heart attacks, liver failure, kidney failure and other drug related causes. The drugs affected their internal organs along with their facial features. This is something my family knows first hand, we have seen numerous kids endure these problems, or die from their drug usage.

FIFTEEN

THE OIL—ECONOMY ISSUE

#14) the oil and fuel economy issue has been around for a long time, wanting for a solution. Washington has not addressed it, and I'm not sure why they have not. The basics of it are reasonably simple, if you get more mileage from a gallon of fuel, you use less fuel. What is complicated about that? It has been said many times, many ways; increase the mileage of the automobile, and the use of foreign oil will be reduced proportionally. Finally after wasting 20–30 years Washington has passed legislation that says, the automobiles must average 35 miles per gallon of fuel. What took this long for it to happen? The answer is the same, money $$$ it's that simple. Washington does not give up easily when money $$$ is involved. Whenever they handle money$$$ about 1/3 of it disappears. This means if less is handled they have less wiggle room to mismanage the money $$$. If the amount is smaller, and some disappears it will be noticed more easily, and they may get caught. Gosh it sure would be great if that would change, then a problem would not devastate us. Instead it would be considered an opportunity and solved.

America has an opportunity to shine, by leading the way, with a timely solution to the oil dependency issue. Not with a stretched out program, but with a crash program. We have wasted too much time, it was obvious that this problem was immanent, and should have been addressed 20–30 years ago. The old saying goes, "It is never too early or too late to a right thing." The Hybrid automobile and, the Hydrogen automobile are steps in the right direction, the time line for completion, should be moved up to a three year completion date. If it's good why wait? This program is extremely important, because we are exposed to the whims of the oil producing countries. Should they decide to stop the flow of oil, even though it would destroy their economy, this action would destroy America's economy. It is believed they are capable of doing just that. Most do not like us they need our money$$$, or they would tell us to go to hell. We need to do more to help ourselves. Let's get rolling on this! Why wait any longer? "Stop talking—start doing" IBM.

⋘ SIXTEEN ⋙

POLITICALY CORRECT

#15) the politically correct issue, goes wanting for a solution. We have factions in America that feel we can make everyone, in the world better. Yes they are a minority, they scream louder than the majority to get their way. This has been working for them, and it is time the majority of us, act to stop this nonsense. They think water boarding is torture, do not say a thing about what the Muslims do. Do they think beheading is ok? Freedom of speech to them is saying bad things about our troops, and our President. They boo, and scream when a speaker at one of the schools talks good about America, cheers when the speaker is one of them, and is bad mouthing America. They believe it is ok if their guards have guns for their protection, but feel no one else should be allowed to have them. It is their thinking that we can rehabilitate sexual predators, and perverts. Some of their politically correct judges turn criminals loose, before their time, and the criminal kills someone shortly after that.

If you say something they do not like they will tell you that, you can't say that. But if they say something that is not true, and you remind them that it is not true, they get mad. They have a double standard, they feel what they do is right, and what everyone else does is wrong. They feel they must save us from ourselves, because we are not capable. They will not face the truth! They have an agenda that goes against the grain of freedom, are a minority, and want to control all things according to their way of thinking. Not good!

SEVENTEEN

LEADERSHIP AND REAGAN QUOTES

#16) the leader issue has been a real problem since Reagan's time in the White House, he is the last leader we have had, that worked with all the people for the good of America. He had the common sense to ask the people to support him, and the ability-charisma to get the democrats to join him, when he wanted a bill passed. He was just what we needed at the time, and we have the same need today, because, we have not had a good leader to manage America since his time. Gerald Ford appeared like he would have done a good job, but he got caught up in the Nixon scandal, so all he got to do is finish the rest of the Nixon term. Then we got Jimmy Carter, he was the start of a string of bad experiences for America. Jimmy's first challenge was the Iran hostage situation, Iran was holding 49 American's hostage, and on April 28th 1980 he had our armed forces attempt a rescue. The rescue was ill planned, failed miserably killing eight American service men attempting the rescue. Jimmy did not know what to do, his secretary of state Vance resigned out of disagreement with the mission. Jimmy is famous for causing inflation-interest rates to go up to 18 % at the high point. It was a mess! Most of what jimmy did was just that, not that he was a bad person, was naïve, an innocent exposed to the vicious group in Washington. He was lost with that group of vultures.

Ronald Reagan was elected President with Bush #1 the vice President, this was the start of the reversal of Jimmy Carter's screw up's, and there were many. Reagan had his work cut out, and was up to the job. It is history but he brought America back to its greatness, we were floundering in the aftermath of Korea, Vietnam, the Iran mess, high interest rates, and many other things he inherited from Carter. Reagan was what we needed, pulled the Democrats and Republicans together, and used common sense to get what America needed. What a great one he was. We will remember Reagan, he is sorely missed we have not had a good manager-President since his time in office. America has regressed since he left office. We need a change from the bad experiences we have had since 1989. Here is what Reagan had to say about how to handle things! Ronald Reagan quotes used during the debates when he was running for President, and after he was in office

"Here's my strategy on the Cold War: we win they lose."

"The most terrifying words in the English language are: I'm from the government and I'm here to help you."

"The trouble with our liberal friends is not that their ignorant: it's just that they know so much that isn't so."

"Of the four wars in my lifetime none, came about because the U.S. was too strong."

"I have wondered at times what the Ten Commandments would have looked like if Moses had run them through the U.S. Congress."

"The taxpayer: That's someone who works for the government but doesn't have to take the civil service examination."

"The nearest thing to eternal life we will ever see is a government program."

"I've laid down the law, though to everyone from now on about anything that happens: no matter what time it is Wake me, even if it's in the middle of a cabinet meeting."

"It has been said that politics is the second oldest profession. I have learned that it bears a striking resemblance to the first."

"Government's view of the economy could be summed up in a few phases: if it moves tax it. If it keeps moving, regulate it. And if it stops moving, subsidize it."

"Politics is not a bad profession. If you succeed there are many rewards, if you disgrace yourself you can always write a book."

"No arsenal or no weapon in the arsenals of the world is as formidable as the will and moral courage of free men and women."

"If we ever forget we're one nation under God, then we will be a nation gone under."

Ronald Reagan

EIGHTEEN

A GENERAL DISCUSSION ABOUT ALL

We will continue on with a discussion about these 16 subjects along with many others, with examples of actual cases, and the outcomes. What we individual's can do, to help bring America back from the brink. Yes we are at the brink, and must act before it is too late, time is running short. Bear with me, here we go! Swift fair justice sounds good, but in the U.S.A. all it is are words. There is no swift justice today, nor is there fair justice, in most cases. Don't tell me that the likes of Ted Kennedy, or his son were treated like we would be with the same circumstance, (because if you do we have something to sell you, is junk with a high price). We just cannot believe we have anyone in the U.S.A. that would believe the treatment they got, is the same we would get.

If we believe in swift justice, why do we convict a person we know murdered someone, sentence them to death. Then keep them on death row for 10-15-20 or more years? Here is what we believe should happen, the person killed someone, and is *guilty beyond a shadow of doubt*. If this is the case then why support that person for more then three weeks? The politically correct folks say, I don't believe in capital punishment well let them believe what they want. If a person in their right mind is going to kill another person, and knows that they will be put to death. Don't you think that would cause them to pause, before killing the person? We cannot make everyone feel good about them selves, and we cannot make everything alright. Let's use common sense, and do things that will help solve the problems we have. The elected officials keep saying it costs more to execute them, then to keep them in jail for life. I say oh bull, if we execute them all we have are the costs of a burial. I think we can get donations to pay for that, if our government is too cheap to do it. Or do they want some payola out of the deal? They just don't get it when it comes to common sense.

Then we have the make everybody feel good, politically correct governor of New Jersey. He decided that the death penalty should be abolished, and for what purpose, other then to satisfy the politically correct people. As spelled out earlier the death penalty is an excellent deterrent, for those that are in their right mind, and plan to kill another human being. The consequences are too great a price to pay, and would cause them to find another way, to resolve their problem in many cases. For those that are not of their right mind, there is no deterrent. They do not know any better. They should be put to sleep, if they kill someone also, because they consume too much of our resources, because of the added attention, a mentally ill person requires. What purpose do they serve? Our question is what is the difference, between a mad dog, and a mad-crazy person that would kill someone? If a mad person is not confined will they kill again? It has happened, and will continue unless something is done to stop it. Look, the judges turn mad-crazy people loose, only to have them kill again, watch the news you will see it. These days it seems to happen daily!

We have far better things to do with our resources then waste them on a mad dog-person, or the likes of a pork barrel-earmark, both are a waste. This brings us to how we should handle one of our representatives, when caught being dishonest. When one of our representatives is caught, and convicted they must lose all benefits. There must be a uniform consequence for their actions, the same like we would get under the same circumstances. They must not be allowed to police themselves, this has happened in the past, and continues today. They must be prosecuted, and sentenced to the letter of the law. No plea bargaining here, just swift fair justice, to match the crime of someone that was in a position of public trust. In fact a person that holds public office, swore on a Bible to uphold the law, should suffer a more severe penalty then normal. They betrayed America with their actions. They do major harm to America, when they act to be a self serving power broker. If the lobbyist's were outlawed, and we believe they must be. I believe about 50% of the problem would go away. The reason we say they should be outlawed is, because they do not represent the majority, and the majority must rule. The solution is simple get rid of the lobbyist's, have a uniform code of justice, and penalize by the law, not by a plea bargain. We need to get back to basics.

Too often some crackpot judge, turns a sex predator loose, and then that sex predator kills a little girl or a women soon after. The judges should have to pay the penalty for the crime, along with the sex predator, he or she turned loose. We believe then they would not be so prone, to doing dumb things like that.

Then we have the judge that will rule on something that the majority of the people voted on, reversing what they voted to pass. This tells us, he is saying I know better, and I will rule your vote means nothing, *"I'm right you are wrong."* I know what is good you are not capable of making decisions. My question is since when does a judge, (one person) equal a majority? A judge, or the representatives, do what they want (not what the people want), all the time. They think we are too dumb to know what is good for us. If they want to know the meaning of dumb, all the judges, and representatives that rule this way need do, is look in a mirror, and they will see dumb. We people need to push the issue when it comes to the people that are in a position of power, so they are forced to do our will. It must be *"By the people for the people,"* not by a few for the majority.

This is what happens when a judge, one person makes these decisions. If a few are making all of the rules, without the input of the majority. We have what is known as a Dictatorship, rather then a Democracy. Think about it for a moment, they make the rules, do not obey them but expect us to. This does not sound like a Democracy to me. This is how they run things in Cuba, China and Russia and quite a few other countries. Do we want that to happen in the U.S.A? If we do we are on the right path. Liberals want to redistribute the wealth, socialize medicine, and have the government do everything for us. We want the government to only do the things we individuals cannot do, like put an Army on the ground to defend our country.

We would hope that the lessons Washington has taught us would stick. Because from where we stand it sure looks like, if that group in Washington handles something, it is going to be screwed up or stolen. Waste and screwing up is what they excel in. Here is a good example, of how well they do with solving a problem. One of their seamiest practices is, attaching an earmark-pork project to a major bill. Just recently the Senate promised to "shine a bright light" on this practice. But it turns out this is not what they are doing. Right after the promise was made they attached $5,200,000,000 in pork to the defense spending bill. They camouflage these pork attachments so they are real hard to find. The practice is to imbed them in the bill in a fragmented form. December 2007, Democrats in Washington approved a $516 billion catch all budget. Bush says he will sign it, the only problem, is imbedded in it are about 9800 pork projects with a dollar value that is unknown at this time. We heard it was close to $22 billion dollars.

We fault Bush for allowing it to go forward, this makes him the pork king of all time. He has used the veto less then any president in history. I support him, but feel he should be ashamed for allowing these things to happen. He was not elected to waste our resources. We elected him because we thought he would use them wisely, which he has not done. He and congress should be ashamed for doing this.

The Corp of Engineers (the make work organization) is another example of what our elected officials are capable of. The Corp of Engineers cannot do the things they do, unless Congress and the Senate pass a funding bill, to give them the money to do the job. Let us look at an example of what we are talking about here. First we will take one that is real fresh in our mind, is happening as we write this. The state of Georgia is having a severe draught the reservoirs are running out of water. And unless Georgia gets rain in the next week or two they will not have water. How bad is the situation, water is necessary to sustain life, and without it you do not live. Yes water can be trucked in for human use. The drought is the cause, but Corp of Engineers control the water flow from the reservoirs. Up till now they are running the water from the reservoir down the river to keep a minnow, and a sturgeon fish alive. To hell with drinking water, and the people the Corp of Engineers are in control! We read an article about what they were doing, and said here we go again no brains when it comes to common sense. The government failed (our elected officials) the test one more time.

Let's take a look at another situation that keeps cropping up, New Orleans, the dikes, the Corp of Engineers is the designer of, and in charge of maintenance of this mess. Are they doing or have they done a good job? No! Are the dikes expected to do the job if New Orleans gets hit again? No! Why not? The marsh areas were dredged to deepen the area for shipping. The marsh's acted as a buffer, so the wave action from a hurricane was dampened before it hit the dikes. No marsh no shock absorber to soften the blow, we must remember that hundreds of miles of marsh were removed. This is to allow ships to come in to service the oil platforms in the area. Let's look at another example of the failure of our system of checks, and balances that are set up to eliminate the possibility of these things happening. It does not stop here. Now we will look at what the Corp of Engineers has done to the Florida Everglades. Back some 40-50 years ago they got the bright idea that the Everglades should have a series of canals, pleasure boats could navigate in. This was so folks could have more fun, but they overlooked the fact that to do this, would screw up the entire balance of nature.

When the canals were dug the water was concentrated in them. This essentially drained a good part of the Everglades. This caused much of the wildlife to look for new homes that were suitable. Their home was screwed up by the Corp of Engineers Everglades (make themselves important) improvement project. The year is 2007, and a few years ago it was decided that it was a mistake to screw up the Everglades. This means now our tax dollars are being spent, to restore them to the natural state. What happened when they were drained was so detrimental to nature that it must be reversed. You must understand the Corp of Engineers is an organization that has accomplished many good things. Eventually you run out of things that must be done, now you have to be creative so you can perpetuate (justify) your existence. Hey these folks get big bucks. This Congress just gave them $22,000,000,000 to spend for some reason. You must remember in order to get funded by the folks in Washington next year you, must spend the money given you this year. The understanding is, if you are not wasteful this year you will not get the funding, so you can be wasteful next year. Spend it or lose it!

I know some teachers that are wasteful, so I called them on it. Was told if we do not spend it this year, we have a hard time justifying the funding for next year. The spend it or lose it rule will apply. This is crazy! Washington at work? As said earlier the more things change, the more they keep them the same. Hey if you change things for the better, you may not get the kickbacks. They will not give up these sleezey practices, because like the drug addict, they are hooked, and only we can help cure them. They cannot do it on their own. They must be sent to treatment or gotten rid of. The government must stop this wasteful practice it is consuming our resources, along with the other wasteful spending. Also the Democrats dubbed the spending of the Republicans, the *"culture of corruption"* because they were caught, accepting expensive free trips from the lobbyist's. Come to find out the Republicans are not alone. 22 house Democrats, and 3 Republicans accepted $40,000.00 in trips in September, many to Las Vegas or Florida resorts. During the first 8 months of 2007 lawmakers accepted $1,900,000.00 in free trips from lobbyists and business's. Free trips are not free the organization that paid for them (the lobbyists-business's) expect favors in return. The tax payer will end up paying for these (free trips for our lawmakers). It is no wonder we have problems, the lawmakers are selling us down the tube. The net of this is, the Democrats dubbed the Republican spending practices the culture of corruption; they had 22 of their people doing what they called bad practice when the republicans were doing it, and of the 25 only 3 were Republicans. They justify what they do, by shining a bright light on what someone else does. This does not make sense to us at all, where do they get off doing this?

Who in the hell do they think they are? Do they think we just got off the turnip truck? This is power brokering plain and simple, because the lobbyist or business would not spend the money to pay for these trips, unless they get a return. How will they get a return? The elected official that received the favor will use his or her influence, to steer a government contract to a relative, friend or associate of the lobbyist or business man. This is how they pay for the favor, and maybe the elected official will also receive some cash under the table. The cash might be in the form of an investment, in a development that the lobbyist or business man has a connection with. The elected official will be paid a large return on the investment. This large return will be fictitious in nature, doing it this way will make it appear to be, a legitimate return on an investment. They do this to cover up the payments. There are quite a few of our elected officials that have been caught, doing this among other dishonest things. Several come to mind. The Jefferson case in Louisiana, with the $90,000.00 in his freezer is one. Duke Cunningham is another, and Cunningham is in prison for his offense. He still is collecting a large pension for being an elected official. Can you believe that? A politician is like prostitute, one sells their body and the other sells their soul, one is like the other cheap and immoral.

We have a very serous illegal alien problem we have illegal alien's pouring over our borders by the millions. The group in Washington will not do a damn thing about it. Why not? Because they are afraid they will lose the Hispanic vote, if they do. The interesting part of this is many of the *Hispanics that are citizens, do not want America diluted by a bunch of illegal alien's, anymore then most of us do. They have assimilated, and are now one of us it must be that way in order for things to function.* Let's face it an illegal alien broke the law by crossing the border. This cannot be allowed we must enforce the law uniformly. To do this, means we must send them back, where they belong. Let's not bend the law for illegal aliens, anymore then we should bend the law, for a murderer or a rapist. We really do not need anymore meaningless laws, must enforce those we have. Again our elected representatives are not doing their job. We must change their way of thinking, we can do that, if we dig in, and force their hand. They are our employee's. Let's make them earn their wages!

Not only do we have the illegal alien's, but we have many gangs that are made up of illegal alien's, and they are vicious. Think nothing of raping or killing, this is obvious by the rape, and murders in the news on a regular basis. So how do we stop them? It is simple, just like it is simple to get a handle on what our representatives do. They have to be somewhere and we are everywhere, all we have to do is get together, confront them, where ever they are, at all times. As far as the gangs go, the police cannot do it all, so we need to help them by not tolerating gang activity, at any time, under any circumstances. Now we have the dishonest police also, and they must be confronted, just as the gangs must be. The police are there for a purpose, and most of them do the job real well. We have a few that are worse then the crooks, because they swore on a bible to uphold the law. If each of you law enforcement people look in a mirror, and do an honest self evaluation. You will find out if you are the bad cop, and if you are, then you are part of the problem. Only you will know for sure, we hope if you are one of the bad ones, that your conscience will bother you enough, so you will change.

Thank you cops that are honest, we love you and thank you from the bottom of our hearts, for your service. We thank our service people, we are proud of all men, and women that serve we need you, and hold you in high esteem. Thank you for your service! We all are tempted to take the easy road sometimes. But the good people take the right road, because they have to live with themselves. So if you cannot look yourself in the eye, when looking in the mirror to do a self evaluation. Then change what you are doing, so you can, and become part of the solution. If you are one of the bad cops that have children, you need to ask yourself, if you want your children to turn out to be bad people. Remember that you are an example, for your children they will emulate you, because you are their example of what is right, and what is wrong. You need to think about this, and if you are one of the bad cops. Want your children to be good citizens. Then set a good example. Kids are smart, and will follow your lead.

You parents that have children that are in the gangs must start to pay attention, to what your children are doing. And if they are involved in gang activity, you need to apply tough love for their own good, by turning them in to the police. The gang activity is a one way street, to dying at a young age. Because drugs, sex, money, and bullets are the way of gang life, if you do not believe us, listen to the news, and look around you. Start to pay attention.

We know we have many parents that do not care. They are on drugs themselves. Where are the parents, of these troubled people? We sure hope you get the point we need to get serious about solving these problems. We do not care if you are Black, Brown, Yellow, White Poor or Rich. If your kids do something wrong, be sure that they pay the price for their actions. And the younger they are, when you practice this, the better grown ups they will be. When they do something that is wrong, there must be a consequence-penalty for their action's that is severe enough so that they don't do it again.

Let's get back to the basics the U.S.A. was founded on, so all people that are citizens could be free to pursue the religion of their choice, and free to pursue their dreams. Just remember good things take effort, so work at doing the right thing, and you too can live the American dream. Too many American's are inconsiderate today, look around you. We know you will see the slob that throws cigarette butts out of their car window, or the covering of a candy bar they just finished eating, and worse. We know you have seen this happening, it happens far too often. Look along the high ways, their garbage is there. Stop it! Teach your kids not to do wrong things you must set a good example for them.

Here is a good example of people, that don't care about their fellow man. This person was driving slow we tried to pass them, rather then maintain their speed they sped up to stop us from passing them. Then were laughing like the fools they are. We have had one speed up to stop us from passing them, and when we tried to get back behind them, because we was running out of passing room, they put on their brakes to try to cause an accident. When this happens, and it seems it happens more then we would like to think it does. We must practice defensive driving, because these idiots do not know any better. Someone has to be the grown up, and use good sense.

Take your kids to the church of your choice all people must have something of substance to believe in, *because "without a dream the people perish."* God blessed this country, because we were good hard working, honest, *God* fearing people at one time. If we do not get back to these basic beliefs, and practices, we will surely fail. Now we have an Atheist that has filed a law suit trying to remove "one Nation under God" from our pledge of allegiance to the flag. Also he is trying to have "in God we trust" removed from our money. The fools in Washington are playing into his hands, and the hands of the group he represents. By allowing the presidential dollar coin with the "in God we trust" inscribed on the rim of it. Out of sight out of mind and after the coin is handled for a while the inscription will wear off. The subtle removal of god from our money, next they will say why bother at all! Also this Atheist has produced a movie called "Golden Compass" this movie, I understand advocates the killing of God. It is getting harder and harder to believe what is being allowed to happen these days, in the name of freedom of speech. Unbelievable! *The Bible tells you "denounce Jesus in front of man*

and he will denounce you in front of the father".
God bless America and god bless you lets all join
hands and get the job done, so we stay strong.
Let's get back to holding our head high and dis-
playing our pride in being American's. Let's dis-
play our flag proudly.

Our Social Security system is screwed up because we have every drunk, and drug addict, and
any other person that makes believe there is something wrong with them, on the dole. Along with
many illegal aliens, and people that are too lazy to
work. We have Lawyers that advertise, saying we
can get you on the SS disability roles, we are good
at it. They are part of the problem, along with the
pacifists, and politically correct people that want everyone to feel good. Instead of having them working for a living so they become useful citizens. The
lawyers that get people on the SS disability roles
call themselves, social security advocates. We call
them crooks they are part of the problem. These
lawyers are just another form of "Home Grown Enemies." Our leaders cater to the welfare recipients,
and other people on the dole, so they will vote for
them. Again they are using our tax dollars to serve
their own purpose. Not only do they use our SS
money to support every misfit, they waste it in other
ways, here is how. Since SS was put on budget,
rather then in its own fund like it used to be. They
use it like it is tax to spend like they please, *that is*
one of the reasons SS is in trouble. It is mishandled
by Washington.

These practices will not end, until we get upset enough, to cause them to end. We know Washington will not do anything, about solving the problem. Look at how long they have had to do something, and the problem just keeps getting worse, on their watch. They are not honorable enough, nor do not have the decency, to do the right thing. About 1/3 of the money collected by the federal government goes down a Black hole never to be seen again. It is waste, waste and more waste. This is the one thing Washington excels at. How does this happen? Support for the useless U.N., pork-earmarks, over payments to contractors for what ever reason. Foreign aid that has no return on the money given, and the spend it or lose it programs, for all branch's of the government. The phony studies of flies, Mosquitoes and other useless studies, committees that have been established years ago, that serve no purpose, are staffed by relatives of officials, and are perpetual in nature. Graft of one sort or another that officials get as payola. Let's not forget the bridge to nowhere that Senator Peterson from Alaska wanted to build. The first time I heard about it, the cost was said to be $430,000,000, then it changed to $220,000,000, the last number was $230,000,000, and with the normal overruns of all government projects. God only knows what it would have cost.

Then we have the Central Artery-Tunnel Project known as, the "Big Dig" which opened in 1995. Since then a part of the roof has fallen down, crushing a car, killing one person. This project had overruns on the cost of 5.6 plus times what it was supposed to cost. The actual cost ended up at 17 billion dollars, when Ted Kennedy proposed doing the project, 3 billion dollars was supposed to be the cost to completion. Also we understand there are serous problems with the tunnel, known as the "Big Dig." The cost to repair the mistakes are not in that we know of but hold your hat they will be astronomical we're sure. Like president Reagan said "the closest thing to perpetual life is a government committee." Just remember only a few of the dishonest officials get caught, because those that are dishonest have many years of experience at covering it up. They have been in office too long, this makes them good at hiding things. Also this builds a case for term limits, so they cannot cause too much damage. Now isn't this a hell of a way to feel about our leaders? But if you look at the results, what is being said is true, based on what they have accomplished, when in office. They need to get real honest, and serous, if our faith in them is to be restored. We're not sure who they think they are fooling. The waste is so obvious we see it also some of us have friends that work in the government. So we hear about what they do, they cannot hide the truth.

We need the 10 commandments back in our schools, and lives so our children are taught a good, moral way of life. Like it is now TV teaches them, most of the children spend more time watching TV, then any other activity. And you know most of what is on the screen, is Hollywood trash with sex, shoot em up scenes, and other demented acts, that are beyond your wildest imagination. It is absolutely crazy, that we allow this nonsense to happen, in the name of freedom of speech. This trash does not complement the freedoms we have, but instead dilutes them. This makes what America does a joke, to the rest of the world. Today December 5th there was a teenage madman, that we believe was taught by Hollywood, how to do what he did. Which was to shoot, and kill 8 people and him self, for a total of 9 people dead, and 15 injured. This happened in Virginia at the collage. Where do these kids get these ideas? From Hollywood! If you watch some of what is on the tube, you will see, the shoot em up bang em up, Hollywood movies. All you need to do is watch an Arnold Schwarzenegger movie and you will see where this trash comes from. He is not the only one guilty of doing the, bang em up, shoot em up, movies that are bad for our kids. The politically correct say, a gun is the cause of the shootings let's look at what a gun is in real terms.

A gun is simply a piece of steel, an inanimate object it cannot do a damn thing. And if you want to find out if this is true, simply load one, lay it on the ground where no one can get near it. All it will do is rust, that's it. For something to happen, some one has to pick it up, and shoot it. Let's take this a step further we will lay a piece of steel 1 inch square by 18 inch's long on the ground. It just lay's there, like the gun, unless some one comes along, picks it up, and beats some ones brains in with it. Hmm this makes both pieces of steel equally dangerous, doesn't it? The 2nd amendment protects the right to carry the gun, but not the piece of steel. So let's ban all steel that fits certain dimensions, or is this too radical? Let's get back to basics, when I was a kid we all had guns when we were 8-10 years old, and we never shot anyone. It seems to me we need to get some common sense, so our kids are raised, and taught to conduct themselves in a good moral way. Hollywood needs to operate to a set of standards, where they cannot make this trash, than our kids will not be exposed to it. When does this madness stop?

It will only stop when people get up in arms about it, haven't you had enough? When we say up in arms, we mean get mad enough to make our elected officials understand what we want, by making them uncomfortable wherever they are, until they do our bidding. *"Again by the people for the people"* not by a few for the many, the majority are not doing the job, that needs to be done, to solve the problems in Washington. It is already known, the group that we have there, will not do the job, unless they are forced to. It is a damn shame that they think they are immune to everything, can crap on us at will, and we will just make believe, that what is happening is not so. They just don't get it! Let's get our heads out of the sand, and address these problems, because they will not go away, unless we cause them to.

Free trade like it is now, means that other countries can use our markets, as they please, and by flooding the market in our country, with cheap inferior products, they put our companies out of business. We lose our jobs in the U.S.A. to the cheap labor, or slave labor of China, and other countries. This happens in the name of free trade? We cannot believe America joined the W.T.O. (worse thing organization), so we could expedite the destruction of the U.S.A. We're for free trade, with an approach that is equitable and fair for both parties. The way it is structured now it is biased, not good for the U.S.A. at all. We bet if the truth were known, many of our greedy people in Washington, are getting paid off to allow that to happen. Heck Clinton was renting the Lincoln bedroom in the White house, to whoever would pay the $100,000.00, or whatever it was for a night. If the truth were known, we believe that is just a smaller part of what the Clintons were doing that is wrong. Then you have Hillary Rodham Clinton, or if it suits her needs better, it is Hillary Clinton. She is up and down like a yoyo because, she changes what she says, depending on what she thinks her audience wants to hear. This is not very good leadership material at all. Like she said "I have a million ideas for America, but America cannot afford all of them." We can just imagine what these ideas are. We're sure they all lead, down the road to socialism in one form or another. No thanks Hillary, whoever you are most of us don't want you for our President.

We're for free trade but with some checks and balances so that it is fair. Here is what we should do; we should have a zero balance of payments formula. This way neither country would have an unfair advantage, over the other. It would look like this in practice. There would be no duties or tax, on products from either country. Whatever is agreed is the same for both participants. The products must meet the standards of the receiving country, both for *sanitation, and quality.* The reason I say sanitation is, I have been in many of the countries we are getting products from. Sanitation is not their good suite, and if the products are not cleaned properly they could carry germs. The germs could make us sick, or spread epidemics. Either country could export any amount of product to the other, with the balance of payments at zero plus 5 %. When the balance reached the plus 5% limit, the offending country could not send anymore product, to the other country, until things were back at the minus level. Heck it is only fair. America cannot continue to support the world like we have been doing. If we continue soon they will own us. Take a look at what is being said here, it is simple, if you have a mortgage on your house, the lender must be paid or he will own your house. In this case the U.S.A. must pay the mortgage holder, or they will own the U.S.A. and our elected officials have us with a very large mortgage. Too large for comfort!

Yes there will be some countries that we must help, but the help must be in a form with limits. This way they will they learn how to help themselves. In other words we must teach them how to fish, so they can catch their own fish. Rather then just keep catching fish to feed them, we must make them self sufficient. This only makes sense otherwise it is welfare plain and simple. We have come from a position of creditor nation to debtor nation. One day the debt will have to be paid. Also we think that any American company that moves out of the U.S.A., and ships product back to the U.S.A. must be taxed, like they are still in the U.S.A. We believe this must be done so they have an incentive to stay in the U.S.A. In the event they still choose to move to another country, this would give them the cheap-slave labor advantage, which would make their products cheaper. At least we would get the tax from them just like they were located in the U.S.A. This would help offset some of the lost, revenue they caused with their move. Our tax base must be kept intact, to pay for the municipal services. They would also come under the Zero balance of trade rules, any other company from another country would. It sure seems fair to me, now we have leveled the playing field when it is done this way.

We have a real problem with our leaders letting China use our markets, so they have the money to build their war machine. They can use this to beat us on the head with. What in the hell is wrong with our leaders? I just found out that China promised we could anchor several of our ships in Hong Cong harbor, for thanksgiving. This way some of our military could enjoy thanksgiving dinner with their families. China said no, at the last minute, after most if not all of the families had already flown to Hong Cong, and were waiting for the ships to dock. This is our friend? We let them use our markets, what in blazes is going on? Watch out for this one, don't turn your back!

Now we must take a look at Barack Obama, using a church on a Sunday to campaign, I guess that separation of church and state is for the people not the politicians. So what else is different? What more can we expect out of people that are Career Politician's. *A Christian* does not go to church, to try to benefit them selves, particularly when they are in a position like that. At least they do not if they have good sense. *"Church is to honor our lord and savior Jesus Christ, not for any other reason."* Oh well, so we have another less then desirable person, an offering for our leader. If by some strange happening he is, elected is he naïve like Carter was? We need a strong person that has the common sense, to ask the people for help, and with enough Charisma, to be able to gather the rest of Washington up, as a group, a team, to do the right things for America.

The only good part of this is we feel he does not stand a chance of being elected. Obama was raised a Muslim? This is what Hillary Clinton's campaign workers had posted on the internet, they have since resigned. Is this true? If it is we don't need him as our President, if not true we don't need Hillary, we really don't want her as President regardless. A Note; the Koran does not separate church and state but instead see's them as one. The Muslim laws are taken from the Koran, they are called Islamic law. Obama does not believe he needs to show allegiance to America? Again this is something of a questionable nature that has been circulating on the Internet. How does one sort this crap out, and who is doing this? If any of this has a remote chance of being true, what could we expect if by some strange accident he became President? Remember a politician is like a Chameleon, they can change colors depending on their mood also. We understand Barack Obama used his office, to increase his net worth. He was involved in a biased real estate deal in Chicago. This made him large sums of money it is understood by us that the return was 10 to 1 in a short period of time. Hey Obama, let me know about the next one, this is good action, if this is true? This makes him one of the dishonest power brokers. In other words he is dirty, like most of the rest of them, if true? We don't need that kind of a person as our leader. We feel he is not capable of doing the job. Because he has no track record that says, he can run a business, we don't see how he can manage the federal government. The only experience he has is as a politician, we need a real leader, one that can run a large business successfully, keeping us in the black, and reducing the large credit card debt that those in Washington have run up. We do not need someone that was part of the cause of that debt. We sure do not want another wind bag we already have enough of them in Washington. In our humble opinion, with our country being founded on Christian principles, we feel it is a big mistake, trying to separate church and state. Why do we say that? Christianity is the glue that bound us together *"all for one and one for all."*

As it stands right now we are a fragmented, divided mess. We do not have a single belief that binds us. If we stay divided *"we will all hang separately"* we are playing into the hands of the enemy, so we best get our act together. *This is worth repeating if we keep bickering, and stay "divided we will surely all hang separately", because "united we stand divided we fall", remember this well, because it is true.* We sure hope you take this seriously, divided countries fail, and always have, the saying goes *"united we stand divided we fall", another truism is "divide and conquer", division causes confusion, and confused countries are easy to conquer.* The moral of the story is, let us be united as a nation, but we still need good honest, moral, and strong leadership, in order for this to happen. Whoever it is must display their loyalty, to America openly. We need to clean up Hollywood, and Washington, they both need the proverbial bath. Because they are dirty, and have been for far too long.

Up to this point we have not talked about the news media. But we must, they are part of the problem, or in the case of FNC, part of the solution. First let's talk about the good part, of the news FNC Bill O Reilly. FNC represents just what they say fair, and balanced. If you do not believe this simply turn on ABC, CBS, CNN or NBC, and listen to them. They rant about how bad the Iraqi war is going, and how bad Bush is doing. All four of them will not report a single good thing that happened in Iraqi, or that Bush has done. And there are quite a few good things happening. Yes there are many things happening that are not good also, responsible reporters, report both sides of a story. The liberal stations parrot the liberal politician's many of them say the war is lost. They would rather see the U.S.A. lose because, with their distorted thinking, without any common sense or for-thought. They believe all would be better, if we buried our heads in the sand like we tried to do before the 2nd world war. Burying our head in the sand-making believe everyone will love us, if we just do nothing is crazy. It didn't work during Hitler's time and it will not work now.

The liberals believe we are the problem, not the radical Islamist's. They believe we are causing them, to want to kill us. Acting this way they (the liberals) give aid, and comfort to the radicals that want to kill us. To the radicals the liberals are like cheer leaders, encouraging them to work harder at killing us. We think the best way to explain the liberal way of thinking is, to tell you about a situation. We were involved in, a discussion with a liberal, about the 2nd world war. Asked him what he knew about Pearl Harbor. When we found out he did not know, about what happened at Pearl Harbor. We explained that the Japanese invaded Pearl Harbor, and bombed the heck out of it. He said what did we do to cause them to bomb us? Can you believe that? I almost lost it, because it was unbelievable to me.

If you want to hear the good news about what is taking place in Iraqi, all you need to do is talk to some of the soldiers that return from there. They will tell you about how most of the Iraqi people want freedom, how they are grateful for our soldiers help. You will not hear this from the liberal broadcast stations. Yes we will have some of the liberals that are

113

soldiers, and some of them will be negative about things also. Thank *God* they are a small number of the total. You will also have some of the weekend soldiers that loved it, when they could spend a few weekends each year in training. This would get their schooling paid for, plus they would get some easy money. Then when they were asked to protect America, which was part of the deal they committed to. They started gripping, some of them said to me. I thought we would never have to be involved in any conflict. What did they think they were in, the boy scouts? They were training for this very purpose. Thank *God* that these grippers represent the minority.

I served my time in Korea, after the cease fire was in effect, late 1954, all of 1955 and early 1956. I have the only acceptable discharge, an Honorable discharge. I received my Honorable discharge in 1962 my obligation was for 8 years. I served 2 years active duty, mostly in Korea, and 6 years in the control group of the active reserves. I feel every man, and with our liberal society, every woman should serve also. The women should not serve in combat, unless they volunteer for combat service. The women could handle most of the duties in to days Army, it is Hi-Tech and requires more brains then brawn. The army I served in the 1950s was an army of numbers (grunts), we were called, I served in the field for about 4 months, became a cook, the food was horrible in our outfit. This all changed after I became a cook. I could cook about the same time I learned to crawl. After I became a cook, every soldier in our outfit could not believe they were being served the same food like before. The only difference being a little seasoning, and a change in the temperature, and time. My point is the soldiers still need to eat. Women generally are better cooks then men. Many administrative positions are available, for the women that do not volunteer for field service.

If every person serves two years after they are 18. America would have a trained force that would only need a refresher coarse to be deployable. This also would serve as a reminder that freedom is not free. This would give our youngsters a chance to find themselves maybe they would have a better appreciation, of what America is all about. Then they would be become better citizens. *God* only knows our youngsters need to find a purpose in life, rather then just watching TV, playing games, and eating. We're not talking about all of our children, just those that do this. They eat too much, do not get involved in any activity, watching TV, and eating are not activities. Just so you do not misunderstand me, we are talking about those kids that waddle when they walk, are too lazy to get involved in any activity. All you need to do to find out for your self, if what is being said is true, is sit on a bench at a shopping mall. Spend an hour, observing the people, and you will understand better what is being said here. Also if you pay attention, you will find out that many parents are, out living their children today. Because, if you do not use it you lose it and many kids are losing it today. That is a greater number are dying of heart attacks, and other obesity related disease's, at very young ages. The reason for this is the kids don't exercise, which causes the body to function well. Use it or lose it, and many are losing it these days. We do have some kids that have medical problems, and cannot help that they are over weight. Do not be offended, God bless you, we love you. The whole thing is upside down, when it comes to our kids doing the right things. The truth is most young American's are lazy. If you don't believe me, just try to get one to work for you. You will find out that what is being said here is true, the irony of it is, it is not their fault, it is the parents fault for allowing it to happen. It is also the fault of the leaders for passing laws, which blame the parent when they discipline a child in any way, other then talking to them. Plus there are not enough fathers that are present in the households today. *Too few fathers have the decency to do the right thing these days. A real man supports the children he fathered, anything less than that is a worthless dog.* This is a major problem today. Enough of that lets move on to the next subject.

We are the, I-Me society we have become self serving, inconsiderate, and most Americans could give a damn less, about his or her fellow human being. If you watch the news you will see, and hear the horror stories about the man that was beat senseless, with people standing around not lifting a finger to help. This happened in New York City in 2007, it was on the news he was beaten with baseball bats. In fact they turned their backs on the scene, so they could make believe it was not happening. Talk about burying your head in the sand, they had to be politically correct people. We hope a real American, a *God fearing American,* if one was present would intervene, and try to stop the madness. Back some years ago about 10 people I worked with were having a discussion. Several of them said *"do whatever you want if it makes you feel good to hell with everyone else or what they think you have to feel good about yourself".* I will not repeat the sick kinds of things they were saying, because they were perverted. I could not believe my ears, and said your thinking is distorted! This was how I was introduced to liberals, and liberal thinking, believe me it has gotten worse since then.

Just watch the news and you will see Murtha, Pelosi, Obama, good old Ted, Reid, and many others who did not. Will not denounce move on dot org for their trying to discredit General Petraeus. This is just plain sick, and we feel they should go see a shrink, because they are troubled souls. The crux of all is, they bad mouth our service men in the in the name of freedom of speech, the first amendment. They want to forget the, second amendment, because it pertains to the right to bear arms which they disagree with. Talk about a confused bunch with a set of double standards. There are three words that come to mind when we talk about this group, they are Demented, Delusional, and Ludicrous. When an elected official does not support his-her own government, and the service men, and women in a time of war it is wrong. War is hell, and we must not take entering one lightly, but when we do, all Americans must support our troops, and our government. We must not act like the group of elected officials mentioned. We feel they should be tried for treason, and treated like a supporter of the enemy. Their actions are aiding, and abet-ting the enemy. We must support the men, and women of our armed forces, above all else. These people that are badmouthing our service men and women are our leaders. I ask then, what can be expected from our youth? If this is the example they see, and are expected to follow? No wonder we have a prob-lem.

All one need do to understand what most of our leader's amount to is, look at the likes of Larry Craig, Foley, Congress man Kennedy, and how many of the others conduct themselves. This is how they behave when they are supposed to be doing what they call "the peoples business." We mention Larry Craig, Foley and the Kennedy kid, because they represent too many of those we have in Washington. This is a good example of what we can expect out of them. What a bunch of confused individual's. If you don't believe us, just follow the activity of the Congress, and the Senate for a short period of time. You will see the most ineffective or-ganization in the entire world, other then the UN. We must remember during the Clintons time, they had a poor example to follow. Bill was more inter-ested in his sex life, then running the country. Most of them do not show up for work about ½ of the time. And when they do they spend most of their time debating, bickering, and trying to find ways to make each other look bad. That is, when they are not busy looking, for ways to attach a pork barrel project of their liking to a major bill. They do this so they can waste more of our resources, or buy votes with our tax dollars we send to Washington.

If we take a look at what is happening, we would be better off if they stayed home most of the time. We feel if you were to gage them on what they do, or if they were to self evaluate, to see if they are honest. We believe only a few would pass muster. Here is how this should be done. Each of them should sit in front of a mirror, and look themselves in the eye, ask themselves did I ever attach a pork barrel project, to a major bill? Did I ever use my influence, to get a bill passed because a lobbyist, offered me favors for doing so? If the answer is yes, then they are looking at a part of the problem, they are it! We feel if the truth were known, and you put up a hand, to count the number of those that would pass muster, you would not need, all 5 fingers. And just possibly you would not need a single one. Can we prove this? No! Do we need to? No. These folks are our "Home Grown Enemies," because they do not do the right thing, for America. Instead of doing the job we hired them to do, they spend their time power brokering, for their own gain. We can see by what they do, or don't do, that there is a major problem in Washington, and they are it. They know who they are, if they have a conscience, they would change, and become an American for America. Instead of being a self serving Dog, that is, part of the problem.

We must have American's for America, as our leaders. Also we must get back to our Christian base. Then our kids will have something good to believe in. The 10 commandments should be used to teach them, so they have good moral standards to gage their activity by. *God* will bless America, if we do not turn our back on him. Let's turn the corner, the 10 commandments are not only for our court rooms, and judges, they are for us too. As we understand it most judges chambers have the 10 commandments hanging on the wall, and in the court rooms. Let's get the 10 commandments back in the schools. This way we can have a standard code of ethics to teach our kids. Let's pledge allegiance to the flag in our schools, before class so our kids learn loyalty to the U.S.A. When I went to school we recited the Lord's Prayer, immediately after pledging allegiance to the flag before classes. We knew where we stood, and if we forgot our parents would remind us, before we had a chance to get out of line. Discipline was swift, fair with love, and had a bit of a sting to it. It was applied on the fat part of the butt, where it must be, so a child is not injured. Not like some of these crazy, parents of today, that hit their kids where ever, and with whatever.

Follow some of the abuse cases like I have, you will see what abuse is, and what you see, will shock you. If you are interested simply contact your local police department, and inquire about child abuse cases. Explain your reason, and most, if not all will show you pictures of what I'm talking about. I sure hope you have a tough stomach, if you see what I saw you will need it. If our children are raised to a good standard, when they become grown people, they will bring with them the same standards. This will carry over into whatever they are involved in, as American citizens. This would give those that went to Washington, something good to gage their behavior by. We feel if the kids are taught discipline, when they are being raised, it will carry over into their behavior as grownups. Wouldn't that be neat, if the people in Washington knew how to conduct them selves? Being honest, *God fearing citizens,* rather then what we see now? America would be back on track, and once again be the wonderful place it was, before we became corrupt, and self serving. A country where it is, *"one for all and all for one,"* bound together for a common cause, with a strong belief in *God,* and the freedom to worship like we please. This was the very reason our founding fathers broke away from the old country, for *"without a dream the people perish."*

We have to cover this subject because we feel this study of animal and human behavior points out, why we have a problem, with most of our children today. Back some years ago an English Shrink studied first animal behavior, then human behavior, in this manner. He had 15 Cow Elephants in a pen with a mature bull Elephant, and 3 young bull Elephants. The young bulls behaved well, and all was peaceful. The next test was to remove the mature bull Elephant, to see what happened to the balance of things. This is what happened! The young bulls started to terrorize the herd, and everything got out of hand real quick. Then the mature bull Elephant was brought back in the herd, within the first 15 minutes things started to settle down, and within an hour all was peaceful again. So to be sure this was not a fluke, the test was repeated several times, with the same result. It was noticed that when the mature bull was in the herd, he would discipline the young bulls, the instant they stepped out of line. This way they knew their limits, and stayed within them.

Next the English shrink ran a similar test with humans, as his subjects. Here is how he ran the tests, and the results. First he studied a stable family, with three children where everyone was expected to perform according to a set of rules. When one of the children did not behave, they were corrected immediately. Every one knew where they stood, and what the limits were, these children behaved exceptionally well. One must remember that Children are always testing a parent. This is how they learn, so it is of utmost importance that any wrong doing is corrected immediately. This way they know what is acceptable, and what is not. If you let an act of disobedience slide for a short period of time, a child will take it as acceptable behavior. Now it will take more effort to correct it.

Next he studied a family with three children, where the parents were lax in their discipline. It was noted that the household was in constant turmoil, which is what one would expect. These children may or may not grow up to be good citizens. The next family was a single parent family, with only a mom that worked. The mom was very rigid, and consistent with her discipline, when she was at home. She was pretty much tired out after a day of work. The children spent the day at a child care center, where the discipline was mediocre. The children had a fair understanding of right, and wrong, and did reasonably well their behavior was acceptable, but not exceptional. Chances are these children will grow up, to become good citizens, because they have a reasonable understanding of what is expected of them.

Next he studied a family where the parents, could not agree on how to discipline the children. The outcome here was horrible, the parents were constantly arguing, about how to handle the children. The children were very confused, and suffered emotional stress. When they were with the mom she had them follow her instructions, and when they were with the dad, he ran them off in another direction. When both parents were home, they were pretty much arguing about how to handle the children, most of the time. The children in this household played the parents like a fiddle, using the confusion, to get what they wanted. What a mess. These children may, or may not grow up to be stable citizens, because they got a bad start in life. Were not taught really what was right or wrong.

The English shrink repeated these tests, with a large number of families from all walks of life. He came to the same conclusion, based on the results from both the test with the Elephants, and the humans. The conclusion was a stable environment with both parents present, and with reasonable discipline, leads to well adjusted youngsters that are happy, and will be much better citizens when they grow up.

Mixed in this test for humans were various methods of discipline, such as time out, losing privileges and spanking. Here are the results of these tests. Time out was very effective with young children, up to about 3 years old with boys, and with girls up to about 5-6 years old. It was established that girls are better behaved then boys, and much easier to discipline. Losing privileges worked well, with both boys and girls but, required a lot of a parent's time. With time out most parents are so busy trying to make a living they just do not have the time to administer it. This made time out a less effective method of discipline, then expected. Spanking worked well with both boys and girls. A parent must use good judgment, when spanking, and never use spanking, to discipline when angry. You want to get a child's attention, not injure them. The conclusion was that all three methods of discipline are effective. Spanking was most effective, worked all of the time, and in many cases, it was the only acceptable consequence for the misbehavior. He stated that in order for a method of discipline to be effective. The consequence had to be swift, proportional to the age, and the misbehavior. The conclusion was that the consequence had to be severe enough, so it was lasting, yet gentle enough so it did not injure, the child physically or emotionally. He stated spanking works!

I know, I'm a product of the time when spanking was a common practice, I was spanked twice, once when I was 9 years old, my dad administered this one. Another time when I was 18 years old, my mother administered this one this one drew blood, my mom started to cry, and said I'm sorry Ken. I told her no mom I'm sorry, for being such a jackass, I love you mom, we hugged. I deserved both spankings, remember them well, and I'm 72 tears old now. One other thing that is a bone of contention is the fact that not very many kids, or for that matter parents, wash their hands after they go to the bathroom. This is a part of the discipline thing, is basic for good health practices. I for one do not want them to touch anything that I'm going to touch. My question is, don't we teach sanitation in the homes, or the schools anymore? If we do have an epidemic of any kind, we sure will spread it much faster, by not practicing basic sanitation. And washing your hands is basic. Doing so will head off many of the contagious disease's, that pass around each year. When I go to a public bathroom, I watch to see how many men wash their hands. Here are the results of the survey about 50-60 % of them will walk right by the wash bowl, without even looking at it.

I asked many women, do women wash? Or do they walk by the wash bowl also, without washing? I was told that more women wash then don't, with the women, it looks like about 70 % wash. The conclusion is women are more concerned with sanitation then men. I just do not get it, no wonder we have problems. I watch my grand kids, they wash if I'm around, or they are sent back to the bathroom to do so. I check it is important to being healthy. A few basic practices taught in the home, and at school will head off most discipline, and many health problems. The discipline must be administered quickly. Both the discipline, and sanitation practices must be consistent, in order to be effective. *"The Bible states spare the rod and spoil the child."* You will find this in Proverbs 23:13 and Proverbs 23:14 of the *Old Testament Bible.* I know the New Testament is more acceptable today, because it is more (politically correct) liberal. This makes it easier to live by, and will make everyone feel better with less effort. Don't get me wrong, the New Testament is good. Just that it has been watered down, by man rewriting it so many times, that each interpretation is more liberal, then the one before it. The New Testament is more politically correct, or at least the later versions. If you want to test what is being said, just go back about 4 to 5 rewrites, and you will see. I'm a Christian, and I feel that way because, the Bible I was raised by is about 80 years old. It reads different then today's version which has been through about 4 to 5 or more rewrites since that time.

We need to use our influence to reform the UN, and at the same time get it moved to another country, for several reasons. For starters it is no longer relevant, it accomplishes nothing useful, has not for a long time, and has no resolve what so ever. If you do not believe us, then we challenge you to tell us what it has accomplished, in the last 35 years. That is of substance, other then spending money, and wasting resources. The real reason we are in Iraqi is because the UN could not get the job done, with its resolutions that were never acted on. The UN is a group of countries that are kind of like Washington. All they do is debate, bicker, quibble, and procrastinate. In other words they do nothing, unless you count being dishonest, an accomplishment of sorts. Why do we say the UN is a dishonest organization? Simply because what we know of the UN, is only what we are allowed to know, and it is not good. For starters, let us look at something that is fairly fresh in our minds. The UN oil for food program, that they were the administrator of. Each of the principles assigned by the UN to handle the contracts, had their hand out taking money, under the table. In other words stealing, some were caught prosecuted, and found guilty. We believe that many, including the leader of the UN at the time, and his son were let off the hook, so things would not look too bad. In other words, a stinking cover up, which they are good at.

If they spent as much time, and energy working to accomplish good things as they do trying to get by with being dishonest. The UN would not have the problems they have today. The world would not have the problems we have, if they would have practiced, preventative-preemptive actions before, rather then after the fact. This is what is spelled out in the UN charter, is the reason the UN was formed. In other words, things would have been stopped, before they got out of control. So here we are, with another organization that does not serve its intended purpose. The purpose is to be preemptive in nature, with the cooperation of all members, for the benefit of the world. The UN was structured this way, so we would have a lasting peace, without turmoil. Now is the time to do something about this misfit. America is spending too much of its resources, supporting an organization, that does not accomplish, what it set out to do. Here is what we should do, #1) Move the UN out of America to some neutral country, #2) Pay no more in membership fees then any other country that gets a vote.

3) Make sure we get votes proportional to what we pay, and if the UN continues to be a do nothing organization. Then not support it at all. That is, unless, we feel we need to belong to an international social club. Please take the time to follow what the UN does, so you understand how wasteful it is. Because we need to make our people in Washington understand we will not tolerate this nonsense any longer.

We need to do a better job with the Vets medical system too many Vets are not getting the treatment we owe them. The defenders of our freedoms deserve better then we have been providing for them. I served in Korea right after the cease fire was signed. Two of my brother's served for the entire 2nd world war, another at the end of the 2nd world war. Another brother was in the Air Force in the 1960s. All five of us served honorably. I feel any person that serves honorably, must be treated with the best care possible, and be given the utmost respect, they earned it. After all they put their life on the line for us. No one can make a more profound commitment then that. I cannot understand why on God's earth, we do not provide the best care possible. We must meet the needs of these Veterans that we put in harms way. We cannot tolerate what took place at Walter Reed Veterans hospital. It is understood that with any benefit there will be abuses. There must be better oversight, so this does not happen again. The whole point being, we need to do the job much better then it has been done, in the past, and is being done as we speak. Funding is not any part of the problem. Waste is!

We can find money to give to the illegal alien's, we can find money for the deadbeats, and we can find money to give to other countries. Then, why can we not find money to help the American soldier? That put his-her life on the line, to defend our freedoms. Look, we just gave North Korea 25 million dollars to buy their friendship. For what purpose I'm not sure. It sure looks like they are going to thumb their nose at us, one more time they are not abiding by the agreement, to dismantle their nuclear facility. Not too many years ago we gave Russia 3.5 billion dollars. This money, was supposed to be spent to cleanup the nuclear waste, spread all over Russia. Also prevent nuclear material from getting in the wrong hands after the cold war. We believe that is correct? That sure did not help. Just look at their smiling, stab you in the back leader, who will do whatever he can to cause trouble for us. We give Pakistan almost $2,000,000,000 each year, in the form of foreign aid, come on now what is going on. We have tried to buy the friendship of many countries, and it doesn't work. Again we ask what is going on, don't we apply common sense to situations, before we act?

Let's do what is right for our defenders, rather then be so darned concerned about dumping our resources in a rat hole. As we understand it, about 1/3 of our tax dollars find their way down a Black hole of waste, never to be seen again. Let me explain what is meant by that statement. We have people on welfare that do not deserve it people are on SS disability that do not deserve it. There are companies that are awarded government contracts because they bid low to get the contract. Then they overbill the government, and get paid. Pork-earmarks are not necessary they are a waste. We continue to give foreign countries billions of dollars that do not deserve it. When the GSA buys products for the government they pay too much (we have all heard of the $200.00 hammers and the $2,000.00 toilets), every project has massive cost overruns. Committees that were formed years ago still exist, this is waste full (but I believe they are staffed with friends and relatives of our elected officials), cronyism and nepotism are rampant in Washington. And if the truth were known, most of our elected officials have their hand out, for the favors they sell. My question, why is it we cannot find money to treat our soldiers that were put in harms way, with the best care available? There are three reasons waste, waste and more waste. Now that we know what is wrong, and who is to blame, we need to act to correct the problem. If we do not we become an enabler, this tells the people responsible for the waste, it is Ok to continue doing what you have been doing. So we must act, and the sooner the better. Here is what we need to do, and we may have to get pretty tough, to cause these debaters, bickerers, self serving jerks, and procrastinators to move. They have been getting away with this waste full way for a long time. First things first, I hope we get a real leader for a President. This is a must for without a good leader it will remain status quo. Not good at all. When we get a good leader this will make a simple process that is difficult to get done a lot easier.

Here is what needs to happen we need a business manager for a President. Why? The U.S. government is the largest business in the world. The President needs to surround himself, with people that are smart about running a business. With military people that have demonstrated their ability, to direct our armed forces. This commander of our armed forces must be appointed because he is capable, not because he is a friend. The President must surround himself with people that are capable of doing the job required of them. Not with political friends, we do not need anymore cronyism, or nepotism involved in our government. We need real American business, and military leaders that are interested, in bringing America back, from where we have wondered off to. This will place us on a sound footing, both monetarily, and restore the integrity of our wonderful nation. When our military is used, it must be used only when there, is a just reason Then we must act swiftly, and decisively to end the action quickly.

To do these things we have to stop spending "like a drunken sailor," and get the SS fund off budget. For those of you that do not know about off budget, or on budget, here is an explanation. The SS fund was off budget, in other words the money was in its own special trust fund, (politically correct name, lock box) drawing interest. It could not be used for whatever the leaders wanted to use it for, it was protected from them. On budget means that it is not in a separate fund, instead it is mixed in with the normal tax dollars. This is the money that our leaders spend *"like a drunken sailor,* and is the major reason that the SS program is in trouble. When the SS fund was taken off budget, and put in the mix with normal budget, this meant that Washington could use it like they darn well pleased. Since that time they use it to support every pork barrel project, or just generally give it away. They consider it, their money to do what they want with it. The social security fund is a box filled with "I owe you." This means that we owe ourselves (the federal government does) whatever the face value of the, I owe you total is.

Our SS dollars are used to support every drunk, and drug user that is considered disabled, and put on SS disability. Heck we didn't force them to use drugs, so why do we have to support them? Also many of the illegal aliens are on the dole. Our officials (some of the politicians) have many of them registered to vote. They feel we should allow them in our country, and support them with our resources. They broke our laws so get them out of here. Take most of the able bodied people on welfare, and the fakers on SS disability, off the dole. Make them work, it is real simple, if they don't work they don't eat. I for one am getting tired of working to support these dead beats. Yes, some will steal if they are taken off of the dole. So what else is new, they are doing that now. What needs to happen is we need to put the chain gangs back in the picture. This way they will be uncomfortable enough, so working is easier then stealing. The choice is theirs we did not cheat, or steal. Why do we have to pay the piper for them? I know that by our present standards this sounds radical. What we are doing is not working, so it needs to be changed. Being politically correct, feeling your pain, and trying to make every one feel good, does not get the job done.

Let's take a look at an example of how a Monkey went about solving a problem. The Monkey was trying to open a nut by throwing it at a tree. After about 20 tries he sat back scratched his head for a few minutes. Then he picked up two rocks, used them to smash the nut, to crack it, so he could get at the meat inside. Problem solved! The moral of the story is, if what you are doing does not work. Change it! Now we're not saying the Monkey is smarter then our politicians, but the Monkey solved the problem. Our politician's have not been solving our problems. You make your own judgment about who is smarter.

We have a good example to follow, regarding the detention of those that break the law that works real well. The Sheriff in Arizona with the tent detention facility has set the example for us. Most of the people detained there, do not want to come back for a visit. Why do they not want to come back for a visit? Because the camp is in the desert, and the detainees are not given any of the Country Club privilege's we provide, in most detention facilities. They are made uncomfortable he hopes they are uncomfortable enough, so they go straight. The hope is they will become good citizens, the Sheriff don't want them back. We need to apply common sense, just like he has, it works. What we have done, and are doing is not working too well. Like the example with the Monkey, if it does not work change it.

Back to Pork-earmarks last night 10/17/2007 I watched the Congressional debates on Pork/earmarks. This was very interesting, what they were proposing (as I understood it) is cutting the total amount wasted on Pork, averaged over two years in half. Then that number would be divided by the number of representatives that there are. This would establish the maximum amount that any one individual, would be allowed to spend on Pork-earmarks. Yes it is a step, that they feel justified in taking. Why not do the job right rather then half way? We will use their reasoning: why do they want to only do half a job? They stated that to cut out the earmarks-Pork, cold Turkey would be like taking a drug addict off of drugs cold Turkey. They said we want to do it this way, and could always go beyond this later on. This thinking is kind of like a woman being just a little bit pregnant. We all know that in Washington the only way anything will be done, is if we force them to do it. They have had years to do the job, and it still is not done. The go beyond to cut it more later on will never arrive. My question is why they want to do the job half way? Why not eliminate the waste by getting rid of Pork-earmarks completely? Eliminating this waste will help solve our deficit spending problem. It is noted; if all waste is eliminated, there would be a total of about 1 trillion dollars available, with a surplus of about 500 billion dollars every year we could use to pay down the federal debt. The 1 trillion dollars represents 1/3 of the tax money we send to Washington. We don't have a money problem we just have a bunch of crook's handling the money. Stop making excuses, and stop the waste. Now!

Remember 1/3 of what Washington gets from us is wasted. If you want to get something done, why not get it out in the open, so everyone can see what you are doing? Come on who do you people in Washington think you are kidding. Stop trying to hang on to failed policies. We must look at how Washington has done things in the past they have made many promises, with almost all of them being broken. How can we expect more from them, then the half assed solutions proposed to try to solve the Pork problem. *I feel what they will do is kind of like an Alcoholic placing a bottle of whisky on a table, where he-she can see it, so they can prove to themselves. That they can do without the booze, resist the temptation. Guess what! The Alcoholic will give in to the temptation, just as our representatives will find a way to circumvent the limits proposed. By trading off what Pork they themselves do not use, for favors from some other representative. It will not work! They have proven they cannot be trusted to do the right thing. Their actions speak for them can it be believed this will be any different? Trading favors, power brokering is what they excel in.* The only way they can make this work is "cold turkey." We believe any other approach will fail. As was said earlier later will never arrive.

If we take a look at what our elected officials do with our tax dollars, it will make you sick. This is the most wasteful bunch in the whole world. We must remember that when they talk about money, they always relate to what they spend foolishly, this way, saying *"that expenditure is only .5 % of the total bill."* This makes the amount wasted, palatable to us in their minds. With the proposed half assed pork-earmark bill they are debating, they have been using an average of $54,000,000 per representative. For earmarks-pork spending per year averaged over the last two years. If this bill is passed it would be ½ of that or $27,000,000 per representative for a total of $10,800,000,000. Is all? Instead of the usual of $21,600,000,000 to them this is peanuts. This is crazy! We (the majority) have not held them accountable. Will we now? At least we have not held their feet to the fire in the past. Let's change that, and put the pressure on them to do the right thing. We can do it! Here is how! This will take your involvement, and it may be painful. The value of the rewards, will more then offset the pain. Because if we can force their hand, to get rid of just ½ of the waste for starters. We will be $500,000,000,000 ahead of the game. Yes the waste is about $1,000,000,000,000 or 1/3 of our tax money sent Washington.

This will offset the balance of payments, we have with the screwed up trade deals, the fools in Washington have made. This is not a quick fix affair, and we will need to stay on them, until they understand we mean business. They are spoiled because we let them have their way for a long time. Just so you understand what we are dealing with. Let's look at something we all have experience with. These people are the same as spoiled children, so we must treat them that way. They will pout, just like spoiled children do when we start expecting them to do our bidding. And just like disciplining spoiled children, we must be consistent in our actions, so we do not confuse them. We must all use the same approach, so the signals they get are the same at all times. Or like spoiled children, they will play us against each other, to get their way. This is what they have been doing for years. Are you ready? These Jokers have to be somewhere at all times. They live amongst us we must ring their bell to get their attention. That means send them e mails, call them go to town meetings, or picket their house when they are at home. We must get their attention often enough, so they understand we are serious. This must happen regardless of where they are, until they do what we ask of them. Because they work for us, we must demand they perform. Anything less than being on the job full time, and performing while there is not acceptable. We demand 100 % of their time. We pay them full time wages!

Yes they work for us, we pay their wages the lobbyist's, and big business's do not. This means these people must not have contact with them. Nor should it be legal for them to wave large amounts of money in front of them, to buy their influence. We must force them to outlaw lobbyist's this will stop much of their power brokering. We must make them Honest above all else. Now we know this is simple, but it will not be easy. They will rebel, so there must be a consequence for their actions, if they do not do their job. The first thing we must demand is they show up for work 100 % of the time. Because if they are not on the job, they cannot perform, and we are demanding they perform. We must remember we are not going to make their job difficult we just want them to be honest for the betterment of America. They will be more secure in their job by being Honest. They will not have to look over their shoulder to see who they lied to last. Won't that be nice! This way they will not have to decide, how they are going to cover up the last lie they told someone. This is because they do not lie anymore. They will find peace in their souls!

We must remember we don't want to hurt any of them, just make them good servants to America. This means we will start out with the gentle approach, and try that for about 6 months. If after 6 months they do not get the message, then we will use a firmer hand for about 6 months. Remember they work for us we do not owe them anything, except respect, if they earn it. We pay their wages, they serve us, is our right to expect them to provide the services they are paid to do. Think about it! When you go to work, your boss expects you to do what you are paid for, right? Why should we expect less of them? Also when a bill is written do the writing in plain English, so we do not need a Lawyer to interpret what it means. Simply write in plain English what the bill will do, "this is what it does, and here are the consequences, if you disobey." No added attachments, no Lawyerly language, just straight forward English. This way a common person can understand it. No double talk, or meaning either in your text, or your verbiage we are not looking for spin doctors. We are looking for honest doctors, so shoot from the shoulder not the hip. We want "the truth nothing but the truth," John 8:32: *King James Bible "know the truth and the truth shall set you free,"* isn't that a great concept?

Just think about this for a minute, if you elected officials practice this, you will be a great example for our youth. Also in following these practices, you will put pressure on Hollywood, to clean up their act. *You got the proverbial bath because you were dirty, they would get one also you both need it bad.* You stink like it is now, and most American's feel this way about both of you. According to the people I talked to, Congress's approval rating is 5 % or less, not 18 % like the news media reports. You are a do nothing congress. We don't want to pick on Congress alone. All of you elected officials are at fault, at all levels of government, and we don't want to forget any of you. Plus if you do something, it is to increase spending, which we do not need more of. Here is a challenge for all of you; cut out the waste, if you do that you will have done a great service for America. There will be enough money to fund everything that is needed, with about $500,000,000,000 left over, to start paying down the federal debt.

Hey folks we have our work cut out for us, but I know you are up to the job. This must start when the missing link is replaced, the missing link, is something America has not had, since Ronald Reagan was President. That missing link is a President, a leader that can manage the Washington spending. Will surround him self with good people, that know what needs to be done, to get America back on sound footing. He will ask us for help, he will need it, to make our representatives straighten up. It will be nice to get rid of the smoke, and mirror approach to governing that has been used in Washington for years. We all must call, confront, send e mails, attend town meetings, or whatever else is asked of us. This must be done, so we get the elected officials attention. And it will require that all of us work together, like a team in order to get the job done.

Yes we will disagree, but we need to use the internet to get honest information to each other. This also can be done, by joining an organization called, citizensunited.org. Or any organization that really is concerned about America, and tells the truth about what is going on. With the circulation of e mail's so we can work out any disagreements quickly. This way we can communicate in a matter of days, or hours to work out any differences.

No, move on .org does not count. This is an organization that is not concerned about America. They have their own agenda it is socialism or the defeat of America, in our opinion. When we start this just be sure you have good security, so we do not spread any viruses to each other on our computers. We recommend, Trend Micro PC-illin for your security, it will not let a single bad thing get through. If you go on line, you can get it for a lot less then any other security program, most importantly it works! It is of the utmost importance we present a united front. Or we will have the same problem, like the parents that bicker rather then agree. Where the kids play them like a fiddle, we will experience the same thing with these representatives, they are spoiled also. We cannot expect them to act any differently, until they get the message. It is imperative that we present a united front, so we get the message to them quickly. Time is getting short. How short? Last week I said I do not think it can get much worse and guess what? It got much worse in a matter of days.

If you do not see what I see, you must be watching CNN. All they paint is a bad picture, so you cannot see any contrast/change in last week to this week. Every day it is the same old bad mouth Bush, and the negative happenings of the world. Bad mouthing Bush, or constantly saying negative things will not do the job, positive action will. So let's shine a little sunlight on this picture. Get a little contrast in your life, don't pass out on me now, (watch Fox News) for a change. I watch CNN on occasion, so I know what they preach. Watch Fox News so you are exposed to another prospective of what is happening in the world. Try it you may get hooked! Fox is as close to the truth you will get, from any news broadcasters, you will hear, and see both sides of a story, Fox is not biased. I also watch Glen Beck, he tells it like it is, believe it or not, he has partnered with CNN, and I still like the guy, he is very expressive with his hand gestures. Lou Dobbs does a good job also and I watch him on occasion. Add a little color to your life things will get brighter if you do. Contrasting colors add spice to life, just like contrasting views will add spice to your life. The reason we ask you to do this is, we must agree, or we are part of the problem. The solution to the mess our leaders have us in, requires that we lead them down the right path. So we must know the truth, it will set us free to lead them.

Since we started talking about the way our government is run, we cannot believe what "Dingy Harry Reid" has done. Or for that matter, that he plus 40 other Senators have signed on to his lies. By now you all have heard of the "Dingy Harry Reid" letter, a copy of the letter can be obtained on Rush Limbaugh's web sight. You can print it out so you have a hard copy, we have done just that. Can you believe it, the "Dingy Harry Reid" letter sold for $2,100,100.00, Rush has been asked to sign copies, so people can buy a signed copy for $1,000.00. Rush matched the sale price of $2,100,100.00. Neat! "Dingy Harry Reid's" lie sold for $2,100,100.00 with the proceeds going to fund the education of, our honorable fallen men and women's children.

With the passing of each day it gets worse. We're not sure where it will lead, all we know, is we need to do something different then we are doing. Again we implore you to act sooner, rather then later. We do have an election coming up in *2008, and it is imperative that we all vote.* Before you *vote remember this, do not let a union or any other organization tell you how to vote. We must get what America needs, not what the politicians want for our next President.* We have had enough of that. Be sure *you vote* for a man that you feel has the best background, and has had *successfully* run a business. The *U.S. government is the biggest business in the world.* The only problem is the two parties, the Democrats and Republicans, will only offer us what they want us to have. This is their demented way of retaining control of Washington.

They really don't give a damn about America. We need to surprise them by thinking on our feet, and voting for what we want, out of the offerings in the primaries. This is the only way we can change

what we have in Washington. We cannot empha-
size enough, how important *your vote* is. We *are in
trouble,* and we cannot tolerate the same old *political machine routine.* We have suffered with for the
last four Presidents *we need new blood, with new
ideas, and common sense. Cronyism and nepotism* just does not get the job done. And *God* only
knows we have had an *overload* of that practice.
Washington is loaded with friends, and relatives,
that are not qualified for the job they are placed in.

We have talked about many things, but now it
is time to give you possible solutions to the many
problems, or all you have heard is air movement,
so let's get with it. We know we have a do nothing Congress, and do nothing officials, at all levels
of government. This means we must crank them
up, so they get with the program. We must demand
they be at work, just like we have to. They are our
employee's, so let's expect them to do, what we
pay them to do. We do not just want them to make
busy work we expect them to be creative. Being
creative will help them sort things out, so they become part of the solution. If they ask, where should
we start? We must tell them, just follow the 16 items
listed at the front of this book. This list is compiled,
a result of their inaction over a period of years. Yes
there are many more things that need to be done.
The list gives them a starting point, so they have a
plan to follow. These items must be addressed they
have been rolling around in Washington for years,
without a solution. Now we expect results. Can we
get results? Yes! How? By making our elected offi-

cials understand, that we are fed up with their inaction. First by talking to them, sending them E mails, or Fax's explaining what it is we want them to do. Some of them will not listen, so we may have to get more aggressive with them.

Whatever is done must be peaceful, but we can picket their house, or their office, until they get the message. We must keep in mind what we expect of them, will not be easy, because they, like us are divided we did not say, nor will we say, it will be easy, it will not. But it can be done, if we all work together. They are spoiled, in need of tough love. We will have to agree on what we expect of them. To work this out should not be too difficult because we have an instant communication system at our finger tips. The first step will be for all of us to circulate an e mail saying what we expect. This may take a week or two, all we need to do is start an e mail circulating that will tell, what our starting point is. When you get the e mail, simply circulate it to everyone you know. Ask all of the people you send it to that immediately, they send it to everyone in their address book. Hey if we all cooperate we can start communicating, nation wide in two weeks or less. Let's get started, so we can see some light at the end of this tunnel. It is my hope that even before this book is in print, there is an e mail circulating. This will open the communication channels.

The next step would be for you to join an organization like (citizensunited.org) or start an information web site. Maybe you could call it, by the people for the people, or whatever name you all

145

choose. The name can be whatever you all want just so it serves the purpose intended. I know there are some of you out there that care about America. Are computer savvy, and can start a web site for us, so let's get it done. This is a plan, and we must start somewhere. This will take a lot of work on everyone's part, but it is doable, so let's get started. *Now!*

Please keep your eyes open for the first e mail that will start the silent revolution. This will start the reversal of this downward spiral America is in. We must keep in mind that we are not a Democrat or a Republican, just American's for America. Our only purpose is being an instrument, used to cause change, for the better in America.

If we continue going down the path to socialism we are on, to find out how long the U.S.A. has to go. Before we have a dictatorship or slip into bondage, go to the web site http://www.libertygunrights.com/Schwiesowlhowlong.html to find out when bondage starts left double click on the link that is provided for this purpose.

The great experiment, "America" is losing its greatness, because we are becoming complacent. Too many of us are allowing ourselves to be too dependant on our government for our needs. In about the 1960s everything changed very rapidly, the result life became easy, too easy! This caused American's to expect abundant life, with very little effort. We allowed our elected officials too much freedom, to do what they want with our resources. This has led to the loss of many of our freedoms, and the downward spiral we are in. This is a natural progression, with the next step being bondage. When we socialize our society, we will be beholden to the government for all things. Bondage is what it is plain, and simple, we are knocking on the door, I for one hope we do not open that door. The 2008 election will determine, how many more years it will take to complete the cycle, from being free, to being dominated by a few. If we want a socialistic form of government, with few, if any freedoms vote for the person that advocates socialized medicine administered by the government and the redistribution of the bounties of our efforts so everyone is equal.

❧ NINETEEN ❧

CLOSING STATEMENTS

If we want to go forward, to clean up this mess we are in. Vote for the person that will manage our great country, steering it down a path toward the elimination, of the excesses of government. We must stop the loud sucking sounds, that take place when our hard earned tax dollars, are sent to Washington. We do not have a revenue problem we have a waste problem, 1/3 of our tax dollars disappear when they arrive in Washington. We have a group of fools handling our money, and we need to get their attention, we need to stop "What's Going On" in Washington because it is the problem. These people that mishandle our tax dollars are, "Home Grown Enemies" and are the bigger part of the problem. They are not honest or moral people by anyone's standards. Your choice will make that difference. We must vote for the person we feel, will best lead us out of this mess we are in. Remember if you do not vote, blame yourself for the problems we American's have. Voting is one of our freedoms, and if you do not exercise that freedom. Then you have no right to grip, when these jerks mishandle our resources. And hopefully we will have an offering this time around, that is a good leader, rather then the usual lesser of two evils, it has been. Like the IBM saying "stop talking, start doing" it is time. Let's all work together to save this great country of ours, America!

In closing, I ask God's blessing for all of us, that we may be strong, so we can reverse this situation for his glory. God bless America.

Enjoyed talking to you, signing off for now Kenneth Hoffman

www.ingramcontent.com/pod-product-compliance
Lightning Source LLC
Chambersburg PA
CBHW060626290526
45793CB00001B/160